LEVITATION AND INVISIBILITY
Learn To Use The Incredible
Super Powers Within You!
By
Commander X
And
Tim R. Swartz

LEVITATION AND INVISIBILITY

Levitation & Invisibility: Learn To Use The Incredible
Super Powers Within You!

By Commander X & Tim R. Swartz

ISBN-13: 978-1606111437
ISBN-10: 1606111434

Copyright © 1998, 2013 - Global Communications

All rights reserved.

No part of this book may be reproduced, stored in a retrieval system, or transmitted, in any form or by any means, electronic, mechanical, photocopying, recording, or otherwise, without prior permission of the author and publisher.

Editor-In-Chief: Timothy Green Beckley
Publishers Assistant: Carol Ann Rodriguez
Sean Casteel: Editorial Direction
William Kern: Design and Layout

Manufactured in the United States of America.

For foreign or other rights contact:

GLOBAL COMMUNICATIONS
P.O. Box 753
New Brunswick, NJ 08903

Email: mrufo8@hotmail.com

www.conspiracyjournal.com

Contents

LEVITATION AND INVISIBILITY

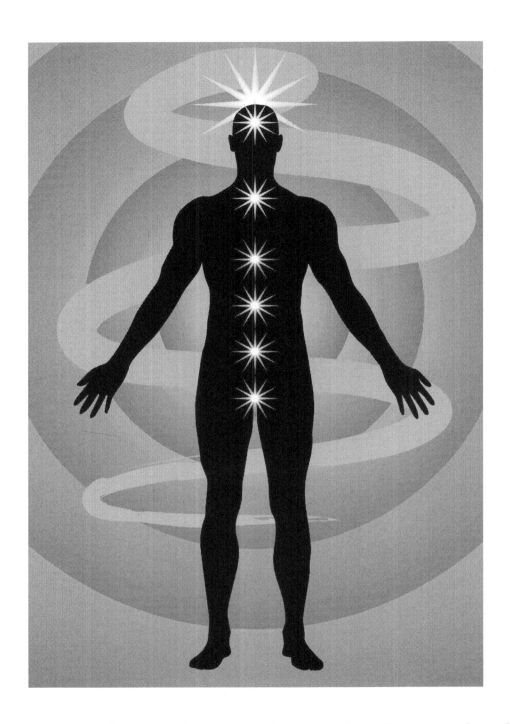

The ancient knowledge of invisibility has been a closely guarded secret, known only by those with the most pure of heart and soul, masters of universal truths and the mysteries of the human mind.

LEVITATION AND INVISIBILITY

Here Today and Gone Tomorrow

Since time is so precious to me, I have to work ten to twelve hours a day, sometimes under very trying conditions. The phone rings, someone is at the door, there is a business meeting or lunch that I have to go to. The outcome is that often nothing seems to get accomplished, or done on time.

If I didn't "steal" a moment here or there, deadlines would fly right out the window, and our little publishing empire would go bust. Traveling on the bus or train between New Jersey and New York offers me a possibility to "catch up," but in order to do any serious editing or writing while on the move, its necessary to "stretch out" and utilize as much space as possible.

As cramped as a bus or train is, it's hard to concentrate or get anything done if you have a fellow commuter taking up the seat next to you. Chances are you're going to get elbowed every few minutes, or worse yet, someone is trying to get your opinion on the Dow Jones or current mortgage rates.

How can you be expected to get anything done under such trying circumstances? Obviously, you can't post a big sign next to you that says "OFF LIMITS: DO NOT DISTURB." Other commuters have the same rights as you do to find a seat.

The trick, as I've discovered, is to make yourself invisible so that those walking up and down the isle completely bypass the section of seats where you have made yourself comfortable. Simply "erase yourself" from existence and have them "move on," and you'll have plenty of opportunity to get some much needed work done.

This seems to work pretty good for me, and I think anyone can learn the process.

The fact is, that over the years I've developed my powers so that when I don't want to be disturbed, I can make the seat next to me and even those across from where I am, completely "out of bounds."

I create a particular situation so that it's as if I don't even exist nor does anything around me. My mind sets the limitations and if I decided to "open up," I can literally "clear the air" at some point and make myself visible to others. Sometimes, if I'm in the right mood, I can even attract a pretty traveler to take the seat next to me and start a conversation.

LEVITATION AND INVISIBILITY

The bottom line is that I'm not at the mercy of others. I've learned (at least to some degree) to set the ground rules. I would have to say that a lot has to do with my ability to make myself felt or unfelt, whatever the case may be depending upon the degree of pressure I'm under.

This is not to say that I can snap my fingers and turn into a cloud of smoke, but for what I've come to learn, apparently other people with a bit more training can take this process further and literally vanish in front of the eyes of others.

There are those, I'm convinced, who are not bound by earthly laws that most mortals have make for themselves. These adepts and avatars, if you want to call them that, have learned to do things which most of us can only dream of.

- They can make themselves invisible.

- They can leave the ground and travel in the air by levitating their physical form.

In this book we will talk not only about those who have performed what seem to be miracles (after all Jesus did walk on water, and he did vanish into the clouds). We will also concentrate on how such miracles can work for all of us to better our lives and to raise our consciousness. That, after all, is the purpose of our understanding and applying the formulas known in previous ages only to the masters. For now we are entering the New Age of Enlightenment, and our "talents" and abilities will soon blossom forth according to our own individual spiritual development.

Interestingly enough, much of what we still consider to be "supernatural" was common place in the past such as on the sunken continents of Atlantic and Mu, and from what we know about our extraterrestrial "Space Brother" friends, levitation and invisibility are performed with the greatest of ease as a matter of course throughout the universe.

Timothy Green Beckley, Global Communications

CHAPTER ONE
THE QUEST FOR INSTANT INVISIBILITY

Out of all the magical secrets that mankind has sought over the ages, probably the two most universal desires would be the ability to become invisible, and to levitate at will. Countless spells, incantations, potions, and talismans have been created, all with the purpose to achieve the goals of invisibility and unaided flight.

Many people today would scoff at the notion that one can become invisible, or fly with the help of magical or occult powers. However, ancient wisdom passed down from antiquity indicates that such "powers" are available if one only knows the true secrets of the lost wisdom of the ages.

These secrets, some which have been lost for centuries, have now been gathered together from the four corners of the Earth. With the new millennium, the time is now right for these lost teachings to be revealed to those willing to take on the great responsibility that such incredible powers can endow on an individual.

But be warned. Such powers can command a high price to those who would use them for evil purposes or for selfish gains. Powers such as these are not to be trifled with. The universe has its own built in safety mechanisms, ready to take down those who would trifle with the laws of the cosmos.

For those who would use these abilities on a quest for knowledge, or to help their fellow man, then they will find their path is readily before them, with guides and assistance to help them along their spiritual journey.

THE INVISIBILITY CLOAK

Scientists are coming ever closer to becoming modern day alchemists by creating an actual invisibility cloak. The invisibility cloak is capable of hiding a tiny object by altering the behavior of the light that hits it. This is the first invisibility cloak made out of sophisticated, artificial materials called metamaterials that work with the full spectrum of light visible to the human eye. The cloak the researchers constructed and tested could disguise a miniscule object, 0.000024 inches wide by 0.000012 inches high — roughly the size of a red blood cell or 100 times thinner than a human hair, according to study researcher Majid Gharghi, a postdoctoral fellow at the University of California, Berkeley.

Until now, metamaterial cloaks such as this one have hidden objects only from limited parts of the electromagnetic spectrum, outside the range of what we can see or for only part of the visible range. And another type of device, made of calcite crystal prisms, has been used to hide things in white, or full-spectrum, light, but only if wavelengths of that light are traveling at a particular angle, or are properly polarized.

The cloak, which works for the full spectrum of visible light traveling at any angle, is made out of silicon nitride layered on top of silicon oxide with minute pores. The silicon nitride is etched with a special pattern of holes. Because of their carefully calculated size, these holes can alter the speed at which light travels through the layer that contains them. This allows the engineers to manipulate our ability to see things.

"What you see is actually not just the light; what you are seeing is how the light is interacting with its environment," said Chris Gladden, a graduate student in Xiang Zhang's group at UC Berkeley, where the work was done.

The pattern of microscopic holes essentially reconstructs the reflected light as if the light never hit the object in the first place, fooling the eye into missing the object.

In theory, at least, this approach could be used to cloak much larger objects.

"The problem becomes actually making a cloak that big. The cloak Majid and I created consists of about 7,000 holes," Gladden said.

It takes about a week to construct a microscopic cloak like this. While the cloak could be scaled up, eventually the time required would make the project impossible, they said. However, some techniques being developed might reduce that time.

Another logistical issue: The cloak must be much larger than the object it covers. Nevertheless, this cloak is an amazing step forward in invisibility technology.

In another development towards using modern technology to induce invisibility, a group of scientists at the University of Texas at Austin have figured out how to "cloak a three-dimensional object standing in free space." That means the object is invisible, from any angle of observation.

"This object's invisibility is independent of where the observer is," says Professor Andrea Alu. "So you'd walk right around it, and never see it."

LEVITATION AND INVISIBILITY

Of course, the Pentagon's been hot on the invisibility trail for years, and for obvious reasons. Invisibility would make plenty of covert operations way easier to execute, not to mention safer for U.S. personnel and deadlier for their foes.

Already, scientists have taken impressive steps forward, and at a freakily fast pace. Researchers in the U.K. have harnessed the mirage effect to mask objects placed behind a device, and Army-backed research is making impressive strides using meta-materials to bend light around objects. Just a few weeks ago, the world's mind was collectively blown when Pentagon-funded scientists managed to cloak an actual event.

The latest research, published this week in the *New Journal of Physics*, uses "plasmonic meta-materials" to make an 18-inch cylindrical tube invisible. Put simply: An everyday object is visible because light rays bound off it, hitting our eyes and allowing our brains to process the info. Different cloaking techniques take different approaches to messing with those light rays.

Meta-materials, for one, redirect light to conceal a given object. But that technique makes it hard to render three-dimensional invisibility. The mirage effect relies on a panel of nanotubes that are electrically stimulated, causing them to bend rays of light and hide whatever is behind the panel. Plasmonic meta-materials, on the other hand, actually cancel out the light scattering from an object. So when coated over the cylinder, they block the rays — from every angle — that would ordinarily make that object visible.

It's an incredible breakthrough, but one that won't turn soldiers into ghostly GIs just yet. So far, researchers have figured out how to cloak free-standing objects from high-frequency wavelengths, like the microwave spectrum. They've still got to tackle the challenge of making a 3-D object invisible at optical wavelengths — what the human eye would be able to see.

"We have some ideas to make it work," Alu says. "But the human eye is not our priority. Right now, we're focused on improving biomedical imaging."

THE DREAM OF INVISIBILITY

Wouldn't it be nice to be able to disappear upon command? Think of all the absolutely incredible things that you could do if you weren't visible to the human eye. You could walk into a room undetected. You could listen to others as they converse in private. You'd be able to visit friends and foe alike without having them know that they were being "spied" upon. You could visit the theater, the movies, a ball game and stand or sit anywhere you wanted, even back stage.

LEVITATION AND INVISIBILITY

If you were dishonest, you could even walk into a bank and walk out with a sack full of money and the cash wouldn't be missed until you were safely home. How many of us, if able to become invisible, could resist the temptation of abusing the power. Who among us can say they wouldn't succumb to voyeuristic fantasies, or theft if we knew we could get away with it. Even murder could become so much easier if the power of invisibility became readily available.

For these reasons and others, the ancient knowledge of invisibility has been a closely guarded secret, known only by those with the most pure of heart and soul, masters of universal truths and the mysteries of the human mind.

Throughout history there have been those individuals who claim that they can make their flesh and bones "fade" from view. These master adepts use mystical, metaphysical or occult powers. They are advanced humans who have discovered various techniques that give them supernatural powers. Some of them have used magick, others have superior mental abilities. It seems hard to believe, but apparently it is possible to learn such techniques yourself. Some say the secret of invisibility can be learned relatively quickly. Others maintain that it takes years of study and purification of the mind. Some say it happens by accident. Others claim that they can make themselves vanish upon command.

Human invisibility has been written about for centuries. Indo-European and pre-Aryan shamanistic beliefs accompanied the peoples who eventually migrated into the Indus Valley in approx. 2,500-1,500 BCE. Here, men and women of great spiritual attainment, and extraordinary powers came to be called Rishis. The Vedas, which form the basis of Hinduism, came from the teachings of the Rishis. These teachings offer descriptions of the rituals and techniques of the Hindu priests.

Later in Hinduism, we find the secret doctrines called the Upanishads. Within the writings there is a section called the "Yogatattva," which gives the rich mystical philosophy of the discipline and theory of practice for attaining knowledge of the essence of God. A serious student of raja yoga was taught that certain supernormal powers, called Siddhas, were a natural outcome of gaining mastery over one's mind and environment, and were used as valuable indications of the student's spiritual progress. One of these yogic Siddhas was human invisibility.

Patanjali, author of the Yoga-sutra, one of the earliest documents among the early Indian writings, described the process to produce human invisibility. He said that concentration and meditation can make the body imperceptible to other men, and "a direct contact with the light of the eyes no longer existing, the body disappears." The light engendered in the eye of the observer no longer comes into contact with the body that has become invisible, and the observer sees nothing at all. The mystery is how this could possibly occur, the explanation of the process of invisibility was most likely left up to the teacher to impart to the student directly.

MOSES - THE GREAT MAGICIAN

Most of us think of Moses as the man who led the Hebrews out of Egypt, the man who parted the waters of the Red Sea in order to drown the pursuing Pharaohs soldiers. However, according to Biblical references, Moses was also a great magician and seer. He was a mystic who understood and acted upon cosmic or universal laws. He was able to turn his staff into a snake, and he performed other amazing feats because he knew certain cosmic laws that were handed down to him by the Supreme Being.

Jewish historians say that Moses was murdered by ambitious politicians, but it may be that Moses simply faded away when the time came for him to vanish. In the book, Antiquities of the Jews, the author Josephus writes, "As he went to the place where he was to vanish from their sight, they all followed after him weeping, but Moses beckoned with his hand to all who were remote from him, and then to stay behind in quiet. All those who accompanied him were the senate, and Eleazar, the High Priest, and Joshua, their commander. As soon as they were come to the mountain called Abarim, Moses dismissed the senate, and a cloud stood over him on the sudden, and he disappeared."

There are those that assume that Moses ascended into Heaven, just as Christ did. However, over the centuries, there has been some debate regarding this issue. H. Spencer Lewis, founder and first Imperator of the Rosicrucian Order, believed that the cloud referred to was a mystical cloud and that Moses and Jesus actually disappeared, possibly into another dimension.

Oliver Leroy, a noted authority on religion says that in his study of Catholic Saints, "It is possible to account for the vanishing of a levitated person...not by the incredible heights reached...in his ascent...but by a phenomenon of invisibility, some instances of which are to be found in the lives of several Saints."

SURROUNDED IN A CLOUD

There is something about a dark cloud that invokes thoughts of mystery. Entire army regiments have been known to disappear inside clouds. In 1915, during World War I the Allies were attempting to capture Constantinople (now known as Istanbul). The Allies had landed at different points on the

LEVITATION AND INVISIBILITY

Gallipoli peninsula, meeting strong Turkish resistance. Some months later, Gen. Sir Ian Hamilton moved new troops secretly to Suvia Bay on the Aegean coast. During the afternoon of August 28 the weather over Suvia Bay was clear except for a group of dark clouds that hovered over Hill 60 about three-fourths of a mile from the front. Despite a breeze of four or five miles an hour from the south, the clouds maintained their position. At ground level below them was another light gray cloud about 800 feet long, 200 feet high and 200 feet wide. It seemed almost solid and hung over a sunken road in a dry creek.

On Rhododendron Spur, about a mile and a half southwest of Hill 60 and some 300 feet higher, were stationed 22 New Zealand soldiers of Number Three Section of Number One Field Company. They noted the strange ground-level cloud as a British regiment began marching up the sunken road toward Hill 60.

The regiment was the British First Fourth Norfolk, several hundred men. The observers watched as the troops marched right into the cloud. However, no one was seen to come out. About an hour later the cloud gently rose from the ground and joined the clouds above it. Thereupon, all the clouds moved northward towards Bulgaria and disappeared from view.

When Turkey surrendered in 1918, the British immediately demanded return of the regiment. But the Turks maintained that they had never heard of the regiment nor had they captured any of its members. Apparently the British soldiers had disappeared forever within the mysterious cloud. Cases such as this have been well documented and can be found in many books and journals.

Recently, a Canadian mystic, Richard Maurice Bucke, had a similar experience. He stated that without warning he found himself wrapped in a flame-colored cloud. For a moment he thought there was a fire nearby, but then he realized that the light was from within himself. He felt a sense of exultation, accompanied by an intellectual illumination. He realized that at that moment he could disappear entirely from this level of reality, but instead was able to maintain the mental discipline to keep himself from vanishing.

Bucke was so moved by this experience that he spent the rest of his life studying it. His special name for it was Cosmic Consciousness. Such self illumination is part of the practice of invisibility. According to many who have accomplished this seemingly remarkable feat, when the principles for how it can be applied are understood, the task is relatively easy.

Basically, there is no mystery about the subject. If we stand in a room that is completely dark, everything in it, including ourselves, is invisible. Shine a flashlight on the furniture and the parts that are lighted suddenly become visible. Because our eyes are light-sensitive organs, they pick up the reflected

LEVITATION AND INVISIBILITY

light from the object and we therefore see the object. Not all objects reflect light. Some refract it and some absorb it. Some objects reflect light and also absorb it. White snow in sunlight absorbs very little light, which is why the sight of it may hurt your eyes. We don't have any trouble at all looking through glass because it is transparent, so much so that people who installed sliding glass doors in their homes were crashing into them until they decorated the glass with decals. The glass in the doors was actually invisible because it reflected little to no light at all.

Science fiction writers say that we could all become invisible if we could bend light waves around ourselves. If no light struck our bodies, no light would be reflected, and therefore we would not be seen. That's easier said than done. Light travels in a straight line. Until we can change that natural phenomenon we are not likely to achieve invisibility. However, maybe we can do it in another way.

HOW TO SEE YOUR AURA

Before we can hope to achieve invisibility we should be familiar with the aura that surrounds us, as it does all living things. The fact that an aura, a subtle and colorful emanation of energy that surrounds the body, truly exists was proved by Kirlian photography. These photographs clearly show the emanations, and it is alleged that one can tell if a part of the body is not working properly by the change in the aura's color and shape.

However, we don't need Kirlian photography to see our aura. We all have the natural ability to see the aura, all we need is a little patience. In his book Invisibility, (Aquarian Press), Steve Richards outlines the procedure by which aura visibility is possible.

You need a closet large enough for a chair. Use bath towels to seal the crack under the door to insure that no light enters. What you want is total darkness. Your left and right hands have different polarities. When you bring them together there is a flow of energy from one to the other. When the fingertips touch the aura is intensified. At that moment you should see your aura.

We don't want to mislead you into thinking this is a simple exercise. It is not. You won't see your aura the first time, you may not see it the fiftieth time. If you stay with it, you will eventually see it. Richards recommends that you put your hands together in the darkened closet just as you would if you were praying, palms touching. Then separate your palms, so that any energy that passes over from one hand to the other must center on your fingers. When the fingers are separated there will be a light produced by the magnetic energy passing from the fingers of one hand to the fingers of the other. An important point to remember here is that when you begin the exercise, will that you will see the light.

Discontinue the experiment after about ten minutes and try again the next day. Some experimenters have tried it for three or four months before succeeding. Don't become discouraged. Even if you don't succeed, the exercise will help to prepare you for the bigger achievement you desire — that of becoming invisible.

CHAPTER TWO
WHAT IS IN THE MYSTERIOUS MIST?

Research of ancient texts and manuscripts indicates that whenever invisibility occurs in antiquity it is always accompanied by a cloud or mist. The ancient Greeks were well aware of it, and Homer and Hesiod mention the magical mists in their writings. In the Odyssey, when Odysseus washed ashore near the city of the Phaeacians, he wanted to get to the palace without being seen. Homer said that the problem was solved by the Goddess Athene, who "shed a deep mist about Odysseus" so that he would not be seen on his way into the palace. As Odysseus passed through the city he was hidden in a thick cloud of darkness.

Enveloped in his cloud of darkness, Odysseus went to the court and reached Arete and King Alcinous. He placed his hands on the knees of the queen, and at that instant the cloud fell away and he became visible. Everyone was stunned to see a man suddenly standing next to Arete and the king.

Homer also tells us that even as heroes were battling over Troy, Hera approached Zeus on Mount Ida to ask a favor. Zeus had his own favor to ask, a sexual one. Embarrassed, Hera said it was not possible, that there were too many gods and goddesses about. She suggested that they go to her room. Zeus had a better idea. They could have all the privacy they needed, through invisibility. Zeus then surrounded Hera and himself with a dense golden cloud, so thick that even the sun's rays could not penetrate it.

Hesiod, the ancient Greek poet wrote about the cloud in connection with the men of the Golden Age: "Now that the earth has gathered over this generation, these are called pure and blessed spirits... They mantle themselves in dark mist and wander all over the country."

Oddly, the English word haze comes from the Hebrew word hazaz, which referred to the "shining cloud that causes man to have visions." Cagliostro had in his possession a letter written to him by the Master of one of the Egyptian lodges. A passage read:

"The first philosopher of the New Testament appeared without being called and gave the entire assemble, prostrate before the blue cloud in which he appeared, his blessing." Blue is one of the colors seen in the cloud, although it has also been described as being blue-gray. The Romans have also been aware of the strange mist which signals the arrival or departure of one of authority. Dionysius told the story of Ilia, mother of Romulus and Remus. She was a Vestal Virgin and was ravished in a grove consecrated to the God Mars. Dionysius wrote:

"It is said by some that the act was committed by one of her loves to gratify his passion. Others make Amulius the author of it. But the greatest number give this fabulous account: that it was a specter, representing the god to whom the place was consecrated. They add that this adventure was attended, among other heavenly signs, with the eclipse of the sun, and a darkness spread over the heavens; that the specter far excelled the appearance of a man, both in beauty and in stature; and that the ravisher, to comfort the maiden, commanded her to be not at all concerned at what happened, since she had been united in marriage to the genius of the place. Having said this, he was wrapped in a cloud, and, being lifted from the earth, was borne upwards through the air."

Here we have a case of levitation and invisibility, just as it allegedly happened with Moses, Christ, some saints, and with holy men in nearly every religion.

Certain Spiritualists are capable of producing this cloud. It has been called teleplasm or ideaplasm, but the name invented by Charles Richet is ectoplasm. That's the name that stuck. It is now called ectoplasm by all students of the occult.

Richet made an in-depth study of the phenomenon. The substance ectoplasm is reportedly produced by the body of a spirit medium. The ectoplasm flows from the mouths or other orifices of mediums while they are in a trance. The mediums can use this substance to make tables levitate, and sometimes this cotton candy like material can even form itself into a human-shaped apparition.

Richet was able to divide the formation of ectoplasm into three or four stages. At a séance the first stage included nothing visible, but there were rapping's heard. Objects moved about by themselves, and sitters felt that they were being touched by an invisible hand. The second stage revealed the formation of a cloud. This is just barely visible. When the cloud becomes more luminous, Richet called it the third stage. At this point, a human nude shape started to form. The fourth state is one in which the complete human body is formed, or materialized.

The shape that emerges from the ectoplasm does not have to be human. It can be non-human, such as animals or flowers, or even an inanimate object such as jewelry or clothing. Before you can hope to become invisible at will, you will have to master the art of producing ectoplasm. Don't be frightened off; it is not as hard as you might think. The simplest way to produce ectoplasm is to imagine it forming into a common, everyday object. Try something simple at first, say a coin or a pencil. Find a quiet dimly lit room, sit and close your eyes. In your mind imagine that a cloud is forming into your object. Visualize the object becoming real. Try to mentally "feel" the object, its shape, its texture. Now imagine it on something in your house, a desk or table top. See it in your mind sitting on that desk or table. Visualize yourself going to that table and finding the coin there.

This experiment can take quite sometime before anything will happen. Mediums have been producing what is known as ectoplasm at séances for hundreds of years in which "spirits" have been observed to materialize into physical form.

Total control of your mind is essential. If you find your mind is beginning to wander, stop for awhile and give yourself a break. You cannot force this kind of mental development. It takes time and practice.

Eventually you will be rewarded by actually finding the object you imagined. Probably it won't be in the exact same place you imagined it to be found. Instead, it will most likely turn up in a place you wouldn't expect to find something like it; inside an old box, or an old coat pocket. Some practiced mediums and adepts have actually produced living beings with their mind powers. This is something that should not be attempted by a beginner; there are all sorts of pitfalls awaiting those who dabble recklessly with such powers.

THE INCREDIBLE PHENOMENON CALLED PALINGENESIS

Palingenesis is the materialization of a flower that has been cremated. A Polish doctor who lived in Cracovia delighted visitors by performing the feat. He had a set of small glasses, in each of which there were the ashes of a certain type of flower. His first step was to hold a glass over the flame of a candle. Soon the ashes would move, then rise up and disperse themselves inside the glass. Then a little dark cloud would appear and divide itself into many parts, all of which would finally represent the flower that had been cremated.

Madame Blavatsky, the famed mystic, wrote about the subject: "At a meeting of naturalists in 1834 in Stuttgart, a recipe for producing such experiments was found in a work of Oettinger. Ashes of burned plants contained in vials, when heated, exhibited again their various forms. A small, obscure cloud gradually rose in the vial, took a definite form, and presented to the eye the flower or plant the ashes consisted of. Oettinger wrote, 'The earthly husk remains in the retort, while the volatile essence ascends, like a spirit, perfect in form, but void in substance.'"

LEVITATION AND INVISIBILITY

The alchemists compared the phenomenon with the Phoenix, a mythical bird that rises from its ashes every 500 years and flies to the sun-temple at Heliopolus, where the Egyptians felt that its appearance was a favorable omen.

A man named Kircher resurrected a flower from its own ashes for Queen Christina of Sweden in 1687. He called himself an alchemist and noted that a person who wants to become an alchemist must have magnetic power to attract and coagulate invisible astral elements. We all have the magnetic power to some degree. This power can be enhanced with the right kinds of physical and mental exercises.

THE ROLE OF ALCHEMY IN INVISIBILITY

We desire to prolong and enjoy our lives, and we look to science for the answers. To prolong life in earlier eras the quest was for the Fountain of Youth. You can still see the so-called answers to long life in some advertising which promises you a ripe old age if you drink a certain sour milk, or eat bran cereal.

Today we equate the enjoyment of life with great wealth and material possessions, and there is no shortage of gimmicks to help you achieve riches. In the past, the love of easy living led to a search for the "Philosopher's Stone," which supposedly created wealth by the transmutation of base metals into gold.

Alchemy is often lumped in with Astrology and Sorcery, but as a science, it was developed at a much earlier date. Alchemists also enjoyed a superior knowledge. The beginning of alchemy is lost in antiquity. Some enthusiasts believe it began with the creation of man. Vincent de Beauvais felt that it at least went back to the days of Noah, who had to have been acquainted with alchemy in order to live to such a great age and to sire some 500 children.

Researchers have traced alchemy to the Egyptians, from whom Moses was believed to have learned it. One study shows that the Chinese practiced it 2,500 years before Christ. The idea that metal can be changed to gold was toyed with in the Roman Empire, although the science did not really establish a foothold until the Eighth Century.

The Church banned it, and all classes of society dabbled in it. Unfortunately, there were some charlatans who gave alchemy a bad name. However, alchemy did play an important role in the history of humanity. It must not be judged by the charlatans who exploited it, but by the men who may now be deemed pioneers of civilization. These hard-working alchemists of long ago were the parents of modern science and physics. They also helped to adorn our literature and art. They have given to our language such words as crucible, amalgam, alcohol, potash, laudanum, precipitate, saturate, distillation, quintessence, affinity and many more. Alchemists often stumbled upon discoveries they weren't searching for. The red oxide of mercury was such a discovery, as was nitric acid, nitrate of silver, the telescope, the magic lantern, gunpowder, the properties of gas, and laudanum. Believe it or not, it was the alchemists who first created the first medical clinic.

It is a misconception to think that the alchemists' only concern was to change metal into gold and to attain eternal youth. Those were only two phases of alchemy. Alchemy is actually the most occult of all occult sciences. The occult phenomena that we find so absorbing today was performed by them centuries ago. Alchemists dealt with autosuggestion, animal magnetism, hypnotism, telepathy, and ventriloquism long before these wonders were named.

Alchemist Abertus Magnus, for example, had the ability to mesmerize entire crowds just as Indian necromancers do at present. Cornelius Agrippa, another alchemist, at the request of Erasmus and other learned men called up from the grave many of the great philosophers of antiquity, among them Cicero who, upon Agrippa's urging's, redelivered his celebrated speech on Roscius. Agrippa also showed Lord Surrey in a reflection on a glass, the image of his mistress Geraldine. She was seen on a couch weeping for her lover. Lord Surry made a note of the exact time of the vision, and when he returned home, he learned that truly Geraldine was crying for him at the time he observed her in the magic glass.

When learning became popular again after the Renaissance, a mysterious sect rose up in Germany. Its members called themselves disciples of the Rosey Cross, or Rosicrucians. They claimed that they got their name from one Christian Rosencreutz. This man was supposedly initiated into the mysteries of the East during a pilgrimage to the Holy Land. The Rosicrucians' tenets were first made known to the world in the seventeenth century in an anonymous German work allegedly found in the tomb of Rosencreutz, who had died 120 years previously.

The legends that sprung up about him bordered on the astonishing. Researchers felt that the society began when it embraced the theories of Paracelsus and Dr. John Dee, who were the unrecognized founders of the Rosicrucians. In any event, the alchemists quickly accepted them. The most important rule in the philosophy of the Rosicrucians was chastity. They could ignore hunger and thirst. They enjoyed perfect health and were able to prolong their lives indefinitely. The earliest document that clearly mentions the Rosicrucians by name and purports to tell the story of its foundation, was called the **Fama Fraternitatis**. Written anonymously in German, the pamphlet was part of a larger Protestant treatise entitled in its first English translation: The Universal and General Reformation of the Whole Wide World; Together with the **Fama Fraternitatis** of the Laudable Fraternity of the Rosy Cross, Written to all the Learned and the Rulers of Europe.

The manuscript probably began circulating around 1610, and the work was subsequently published in several languages. The first printed edition appeared in 1614 in the town of Kassel in western Germany.

Readers who desired to join in reforming the world were invited to "leave the old course, esteeming Popery, Aristotle, and Galen, yea and that which hath but a mere show of learning." The author asserted that no one could apply for membership directly, but would-be applicants might "speak either by word of mouth, or else...in writing. And this we say for a truth, that whosoever shall earnestly, and from his heart, bear affection unto us, will come to the fraternity's notice. And it shall be beneficial to him in goods, body, and soul."

In case anyone thought that the benefits might include lessons in practical alchemy, the author declared that "concerning the ungodly and accursed gold-making we do therefore by these presents publicly testify, that the true philosophers are far of another mind, esteeming little of the making of gold, which is but a subsidiary activity; for besides that, they have a thousand better things." Simply put, the Rosicrucians knew how to transform base metal into gold and how to make medicinal elixirs, and they could do either when it suited them, but their strongest alchemy was reserved for another, more laudable purpose: the transmutation of ordinary mortal intellect into spiritual and philosophical wisdom.

One of the hidden secrets of the alchemists and the Rosicrucians was the ability to make a living being invisible to "all around him." The knowledge to render a man invisible was revealed to a seventeenth-century French traveler named Paul Lucas. Lucas was traveling in what is now Turkey when he was introduced to a dervish, a monk in a mystic Muslim sect. "He was a man in every way extraordinary in learning," Lucas wrote after a long conversation with the dervish.

The dervish told Lucas about the "sublime science" and the quest for the philosophers' stone. The philosophers' stone could convey immortality upon its holder, as well as knowledge to "hide oneself away from all who would seek him." As proof, the dervish mentioned the name of Nicholas Flamel, one of France's most renowned alchemists and one who reportedly had possessed the stone. Flamel had lived in Paris during the latter half of the fourteenth century. He had amassed great wealth and had earned a saintly and enduring reputation by spending most of his fortune on charitable works. The dervish claimed that Flamel could "cover himself with a mist of darkness and that no locked door could keep him out."

Paul Lucas pointed out to the dervish that Flamel had died in 1417 at the age of eighty-seven. The dervish "smiled at my simplicity," Lucas wrote, "and asked, do you really believe this? No, no, my friend, Flamel is still living. It is not above three years since I left him in the Indies," he said. "He is one of my best friends." With that the dervish vanished completely before the astonished eyes of Lucas.

Alchemists believed that the philosophers' stone was a "stone which is not a stone." This substance, which carried literally hundreds of other names, such as the "powder of projection," the "virgins milk," and the "shade of the sun," was credited with miraculous powers. Not only could it help transmute base metals into gold, it reputedly could soften glass, render its owner invisible at will, or give an alchemist the ability to levitate. Some people believed that the stone would enable them to converse with angels or even to understand the language of animals.

One way the philosophers' stone could produce invisibility was by creating a "mist of heaven" which would envelop the holder and render him invisible to all around him. However, a philosophers' stone is really not needed in order to produce a "mist of invisibility." Adepts have known for a long time that with the right mental attitude, and a little practice, a supernatural mist can be formed in order to render a person invisible from prying eyes.

STEPS TO FORMING YOUR OWN MIST

Steve Richards in his book, *Invisibility* (Aquarian Press), states that the reader should consider themselves alchemists with their own laboratories. The laboratory in this case is mostly atmosphere. What is needed is a room with limited light coming in from the outside. One bare wall is also essential, or perhaps a door that leads into a darkened room. Most important of all is privacy. A skeptic in the room will insure failure. The methods are simple, you just need to have patience and take the time.

Sit quietly and comfortably. You should then direct your gaze to one single area. This is important. The cloud will then form at the place that holds your attention. If you shift your gaze to other spots in the room, the cloud will not have a chance to build up. Your effort is cumulative. The longer you look at one area, the more definite the cloud becomes.

For best results Richards suggest you defocus your eyes. Look beyond what is in front of you, as if you are looking ten miles away. Some authorities suggest that you keep your eyes half closed. With this idea you will have to experiment. Some experts say a cloud forms better against a black background rather than a white one. You will have to practice de-focusing your eyes. With a little concentration you can do it. Without it, the technique is useless. Chanting is suggested, but it can be distracting. Richards does not recommend it for that reason. Remember, you have to stare, de-focus your eyes, and then chant. That could be asking for too much. Again, if you don't have absolute privacy, forget it. If you feel that you must chant to help you form the cloud, use the mantra RA-MA, which is the name of a Hindu god and the name of a city where the School of Prophets was founded in ancient Palestine. RA represents the masculine energy. MA is the negative, feminine potency. Together, they are the creative power that brought the universe into existence out of the cloud in the beginning. Draw out each syllable and repeat them twenty or twenty-five times per session. If it works for you, fine. If you get no results, drop it.

Another good chanting method is to chant the vowel sounds, A, E, I, O, U. Chant each sound slowly so you can feel each resonating through different parts of the body. Each vowel will affect a different place in your body. Do this for about ten minutes, don't forget to breath deeply with sound, don't hold your breath, just breath deeply and then let it out with each vowel sound.

Patience is the secret key here. Don't be discouraged. It won't happen that you will see a cloud for the first time; it may not happen after scores of times. However, it will happen if you stick with it.

What you may see after some good efforts is something that looks like heat waves. That shows that you are heading in the right direction. With practice, the waves will start to solidify, becoming more and more dense and taking on the appearance of a slight fog or mist.

If your backdrop is white, you may assume you are getting results when you see a faint blue image. This will look somewhat like the blue after image you see after someone has taken your picture with a flash bulb. One thing is certain, when you do achieve results you won't be able to see anything on the other side of the cloud.

The next step includes building the cloud. You do this by starting with your hands about a foot or so apart. Then bring them together. Think that you are compressing astral material between your hands. You bring your hands together and then separate them much like a man playing the accordion. This technique may work for you, and if it does you are likely to see balls of light between your hands. If it doesn't, try another technique.

One that you may be successful with concerns will power and eye movement. Your hands are not involved. Once the cloud has started to form, look away from it. Permit the energy to collect in another region of space. After a moment, bring your eyes gradually toward the center, where the main cloud is forming. While you are doing this, command your will power to force the energy in other parts of the room to join with the energy already in the cloud. You can glance below the cloud, and to either side of it. Above all, do not strain your eyes. It's not necessary. In fact, your eyes should be passive. All of what you do must be with your mind.

Remember to take a break when you start to feel fatigued. These techniques cannot be forced or hurried. Taking breaks helps to relieve the tedium which too often accompanies occult experimentation.

In his definitive work, Steve Richards notes that you will probably have some trouble with your cloud after it has formed. It will have a tendency to scatter to the four corners of the room. This is natural and is in accordance with the law of thermodynamics. If you allow it to happen, all the energy in the cloud will become evenly dispersed throughout the room. The action of being dispersed takes the form of a spin or vortex. To prevent that from happening, a counter spin must be produced. The dispersing spin is always in a clockwise direction. What you must do is will it to turn in a counterclockwise direction. What will happen then is that the cloud will become smaller and denser. Using this method, some experts have been able to block out the light of a 100-watt bulb. The method has also been compared with forming a nebulae in outer space. Galaxies are allegedly formed this way, with huge clouds spinning and condensing until they form stars and planets. One of the secrets of invisibility seems to be for an individual to wrap themselves inside a "cloud" or mist-like vapor. Entire armies have been known to vanish under such conditions.

At this point Richards says you are now ready to make yourself invisible with the help of your cloud. We will assume that you have a definite cloud with lots of astral substance in it. You must now draw the cloud around you so that you will be invisible. The cloud has to be big enough to completely cover you.

There may be a shine to the cloud. You don't want that because the shine is like a beacon. What you want is something neutral, something that will blend with your background. Use your will power for this, the shine can be suppressed with a little effort. When the large cloud has enshrouded you, look into a mirror to see if you see your reflection. It you don't see it, you have done it!

While you are perfecting your art, you may also experiment with materializations. You might try producing lights in your room, columns of smoke, or images. You should also be able to produce spontaneous sounds such as knocks or even voices.

LEVITATION AND INVISIBILITY

While talking to a friend recently, we both noticed a tendency to sometimes lose things. They just weren't where we remembered putting them. After much searching, we go back to an area we just looked, and unexpectedly, the item is suddenly there.

Rather than attributing these mysterious disappearances to elves or poltergeists, we decided it must be some kind of stress induced "negative hallucination," a condition where you are prevented from seeing something that you really need at the moment.

Mystics have told of their ability to induce a "mental confusion" in those around them. This takes two forms, one of which is a cloud or mental fog which is impressionable by another's thoughts, the other takes advantage of the brain not wanting to deal with anything that doesn't immediately fit into the person's view of reality, such as a chaotic or complex image.

When looking towards such an area, the eye will jump past the overly complex image, seeking to find familiar visual territory that doesn't require a high degree of analysis. This phenomenon has been noted with the Native Americans who could not see the first Spanish ships that were clearly visible in the harbor. Only when someone else described what they were seeing, could the rest of the group begin to see the reality. Almost like a visual hundredth monkey effect.

A Russian mentalist and paranormal researcher by the name of Professor L. L. Vasiliev spoke of an incident where he passed a blank piece of paper to a bank teller. The teller then gave him 1000 ruble's in return. Vasiliev said that he had projected an image into the tellers' mind that the paper was a cashier's check in the amount of 1000 rubles. The money was returned after witnesses testified to the success of the experiment.

Another experiment by Vasiliev was based on a bet with Stalin. Many of the Russian scientists had no patience with paranormal investigations, but Vasiliev and some of his colleagues wanted to establish a research institute to investigate and perfect useful techniques.

Vasiliev made a bet with Stalin that if he could appear in Stalin's private study at 8 PM on a specified weeknight, Stalin would agree to establish a research institute for paranormal investigations.

Stalin was always heavily guarded, even at home, so he thought this would be a sure bet. On the appointed night, Stalin was sitting in front of his fireplace reading, when the clock struck 8 o'clock. He heard a clearing of the throat, looked up and saw Vasiliev sitting in an armchair opposite him.

Stalin immediately called in the guards and demanded to know how Vasiliev had gotten past all of them. Each denied they had seen Vasiliev that night. Finally, before Stalin could have them all put to death, Vasiliev explained that he had projected the image of one of Stalin's most trusted advisors into the minds of the soldiers as he walked through.

This advisor was of such high rank that he was allowed to come and go without challenge by the soldiers. It was at this point that Stalin was convinced of the usefulness of psychic research and funded the highly effective Russian paranormal research efforts.

When I was about 15 years of age, I experienced a peculiar event that left a lasting impression. We had a local newsstand that received new magazines and paperback books once a week. Being a heavy reader, I had a friend who I often met there as we went through looking for books and magazines on UFOs, paranormal, and science fiction.

One night, we were to meet at 7 PM. I arrived first and climbed onto a ladder with my feet about 2 feet off the floor so that I was easy to spot from anywhere in this small shop. This shop also had only one door with an aisle having books and magazines on each side of the aisle. I heard someone enter, turned around and it was my friend. He looked around the shop, apparently without seeing me. What made this so strange was that I was right in front of him, no more then ten feet away.

I was puzzled about this, thinking he had not said hello because he must be kidding around. Prior to his entry, I was very absorbed in a new paperback book that I was contemplating buying. A few minutes later, I stepped off the ladder and walked up to him.

My friend was startled and asked how I'd gotten into the shop without passing by him. I explained that I'd been there all along. He thought I was lying and asked the cashier who confirmed I'd been there for at least 30 minutes. It was very strange. I don't know if he was distracted or if my deep concentration on the book produced some kind of "cloud of confusion" to his perception of the surroundings.

What is the purpose of all this? The answer could be, invulnerability. In the past, man was vulnerable to all kinds of wild predators. In this day and age we are faced with new dangers. We can be potential victims of muggers, killers, speeding vehicles, and other modern-day dangers. To be invisible is to be invulnerable. You are able to isolate yourself from whatever danger is present.

LEVITATION AND INVISIBILITY

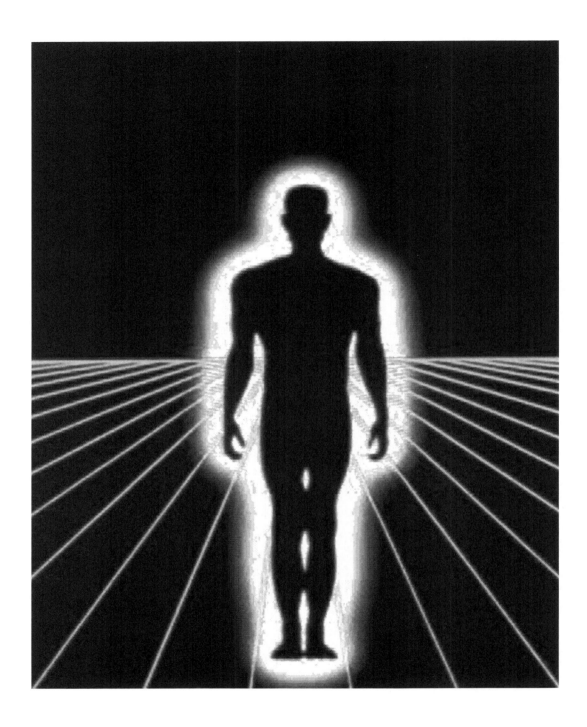

One of the hidden secrets of the alchemists and the Rosicrucians was the ability to make a living being invisible to "all around him." The knowledge to render a man invisible was revealed to a seventeenth-century French traveler named Paul Lucas.

CHAPTER THREE

MADAME BLAVATSKY ON INVULNERABILITY

"The astral fluid can be compressed about a person so as to form an elastic shell, absolutely non-penetrable by any physical object, however great the velocity with which it travels. In a word, this fluid can be made to equal and even excel in resisting power, water and air.

"In India, Malabar, and some places of Central Africa, the conjurers will freely permit any traveler to fire his musket or revolver at them, without touching the weapon themselves or selecting the balls. In Laing's *Travels Among the Timanni, the Kourankos, and the Soulimasoccurs a description by an English travel*er, the first white man to visit the tribe of the Soulimas, of a very curious scene. A body of picked soldiers fired upon a chief who had nothing to defend himself with but certain talismans. Although their muskets were properly loaded and aimed, not a ball could strike him. Salverte gives a similar case in the *Philosophy of Occult Sciences*: 'In 1568 the Prince of Orange condemned a Spanish prisoner to be shot at Juliers; the soldiers tied him to a tree and fired, but he was invulnerable. They at last stripped him to see what armor he wore, but found only an amulet. When this was taken from him, he fell dead at the first shot.'

"Many travelers, this writer included, have witnessed instances of this invulnerability where deception was impossible. A few years ago, there lived in a African village an Abyssinian, who passed for a sorcerer. Upon on occasion a party of Europeans, going to Sudan, amused themselves for an hour or two in firing at him with their own pistols and muskets, a privilege which he gave them for a trifling fee. As many as five shots were fired simultaneously, and the muzzles of the pieces were not above two yards distant from the sorcerer's breast.

"In each case, simultaneously with the flash, the bullet would appear just behind the muzzle, quivering in the air, and then fall harmlessly to the ground. A German offered the magician a five franc piece if he would allow him to fire the gun with the muzzle touching his body. The magician at first refused, but finally, after appearing to hold a conversation with someone inside the ground, consented. The experimenter carefully loaded, and pressing the muzzle of the weapon against the sorcerer's body, fired. The barrel burst into fragments as far down as the stock, and the magician walked off unhurt.

"In our own time several well-known mediums have frequently, in the presence of the most respectable witnesses, not only handled blazing coals and actually placed their faces upon a fire without singeing a hair, but even laid flaming coals upon the hands and heads of bystanders. The well-known story of the Indian chief, who confessed to General George Washington that at Braddock's defeat he fired his rifle at him seventeen times without effect, will recur to the reader in this connection."

Obviously, all of the invulnerable people mentioned by Madame Blavatsky were protected by a cloud made up of astral material, or ectoplasm. It was invisible to the naked eye, but quite strong, strong enough to stop a bullet. However, this is one experiment we would advise you not to try no matter how strong you think your own cloud is.

HOW TO ACHIEVE CLOUDLESS INVISIBILITY

Madame David-Neel explained in her book, *Magic and Mystery in Tibet*, that if you walk among crowds shouting and bumping into people you will make yourself quite visible. But, if you walk noiselessly, touching no one, looking at no one, you may be able to pass without being seen. Animals do this all the time to catch prey. It has also been pointed out that if you sit motionless you can cut down on your visibility.

However there is a drawback to this method. Your mind generates disquiteness. David-Neel says, "The work of the mind generates an energy which spreads all around the one who produces it, and this energy is felt in various ways by those who come into touch with it. The idea is to cut off that source of energy, or noise. If you can do that you become as silent as anyone can be. You may still be seen. That is, a camera or mirror would pick up your image, but you would not be noticed.

Said one expert: "When the mind inhibits emanation of its radioactivity it ceases to be the source of mental stimuli to others, so that they become unconscious of the presence of an Adept of the Art, just as they are unconscious of invisible beings living in a rate of vibration unlike their own."

Aleister Crowley wrote: "The real secret of invisibility is not concerned with the laws of optics at all. The trick is to prevent people noticing you when they would normally do so."

Apparently, Crowley had the power to keep people from noticing him. In an experiment, he took a walk along a street dressed in a golden crown and a scarlet robe. He did not attract attention to himself. Eliphas Levi points out: "A man, for example, pursued by murderers, after having run down a side street, returns instantly and comes, with a calm face, toward those who are pursuing him, or mixes with them and appears occupied with the same pursuit. He will certainly render himself invisible. The person who would be seen is always remarked, and he who would remain unnoticed effaces himself and disappears."

In 1925 Marie Harlowe had a strange experience that convinced her in the reality of invisibility. At that time she worked in a small western town in an industrial office. After a disagreement with a local jeweler over the cost of a ring, Harlowe had to hurriedly catch a train to keep an appointment in a nearby town.

After she had got on the train she noticed the conductor, the jeweler and the local sheriff enter the car she was seated in. All three men came down the aisle and stopped directly where she was sitting. The conductor said, "She was sitting right here. I don't know if she got off or not, but here is where she was sitting."

The conductor was anxious to get the train going, and the other two men got off the train, mumbling about looking for her in the train station. While the men were close to Harlowe in the train aisle, the conductor stood on her foot, leaving a dirty smudge on her white shoe.

At that point Harlowe realized that she had been invisible to the three men and a half-full train car of passengers. Thinking back, she knew immediately on seeing the jeweler and the sheriff that she was going to be arrested. She felt that time stood still as she desired to be invisible more than anything else she had ever wanted.

The train started up, and the conductor was a very surprised man when he saw Harlowe sitting where he had last seen her. Afterwards, the jeweler dropped the charges against her, admitting that he had been trying to swindle her out of some extra money.

Since that involuntary experience of making her physical body invisible, Marie Harlowe learned a great deal about the conscious method of producing this phenomenon. A Hindu student suggested that she had not really dematerialized on the train and became invisible, but had only hypnotized the three men.

Harlowe speculated that due to her Yoga exercises, particularly methods of breathing, that she had developed a Will as related to bodily and mental functions, which is needed for a person to produce phenomena of this type. Tibetan Tantra Yoga teaches much, and in detail, about the art of invisibility. It declares that it is a matter of shape-shifting of the bodily form. Through direction of a subtle mental faculty or psychic power, whereby all forms, animate and inanimate, including man's own form, are created, the human body can either be dissolved, and thereby made invisible, by magically inhibiting the faculty, or be mentally imperceptible to others, and thus equally invisible to them by changing the body's vibration.

The mind can inhibit emanation of its radioactivity, and thus cease to be mental stimuli to others, so they become unconscious of the presence of that person. We are always unconscious of many invisible beings living in different vibratory expressions than our own.

The process according to Evans-Wents, who wrote and translated several books on Tibetan Tantra Yoga, is "giving palpable being to visualization," as an architect makes his two-dimension plans three dimensional, but in reverse.

In the experience on the train, Harlowe did not "go" anywhere. She was there all the time, conscious of everything going on, evidenced by the mark made on her shoe. She had simply drawn the shutters (changed the body rate of vibrations).

Those wishing to learn the secret art of invisibility ought to study a little of Tantric Yoga. Madame David-Neel, by these methods, produced a "living" form which stayed with her day and night, in sight of those around her. However, it took her six months of psychic struggle to get the form dissolved.

All of which makes more understandable the story of the Japanese man who meditated upon creating himself as a butterfly form, and thereafter was never sure that he was a man who thought he had been a butterfly, or a butterfly who now thought he was a man.

A SIMPLE METHOD

Sit quietly. Close your eyes. Allow your consciousness to slowly turn inward. Believe it or not, this does not require any effort. It's a natural and involuntary process. The first step is to blot out your environment. Make yourself oblivious to it. Next, keep in your mind the thought that you want to hide. Do this even though you may be sitting in an open room with other people around. Finally, eliminate all thoughts from your mind. This is probably the hardest thing for most people to accomplish, emptying all thoughts from your mind. Most of us find that our minds are almost always working. When we attempt to clear our heads, thoughts and images flood in at a fantastic rate.

To try and clean your mind of intruding thoughts, try concentrating on one particular thing. If you are of a religious mind, try the image of Jesus. Others have reported success with visualizing a clear, white light. While others like to form a pentagram with their mind. Whatever your choice, remember, the goal is to remove all thought from your mind. Remember, thoughts produce energy, and energy makes you more visible. Stop thinking, remain motionless with eyes closed, and you become invisible...not in the literal sense of the word, but unnoticed.

J.H. Brennan has devised a method to stop thought-energy. He says that if he cannot stop himself from shouting, he can conceal himself from you by surrounding himself with a soundproof screen that shuts out the noise. He uses the word "shouting" to mean "thinking." There is a technique for doing that and it is taught by the AMORC Rosicrucians.

THE VEIL OF OBSCURITY

With this technique you can actually produce real invisibility. The Rosicrucians advise you to sit quietly as though you are meditating. Close your eyes. Now imagine that you are completely surrounded by a soundproof screen. Think of it as a curtain hanging down all around you, completely concealing you. Think of the curtain until you can feel its presence, keeping in mind that the curtain will make you invisible to others.

How can you tell if your experiment is successful? Simple. Place a mirror at the opposite side of the room, beyond the Veil's influence. You will be able to see through the curtain, but outsiders will not be able to see in. If you are successful, you will not see your image in the mirror.

However, don't hope for success immediately. Give yourself plenty of time to achieve it. Be patient, and never become discouraged. Acquiring occult powers is not easy. You can be sure that those who are successful are those who have enormous patience.

THE INANIMATE-ANIMATE ASSUMPTION METHOD

This is an amazing psychic experiment that can get you inside of objects, animals or people for brand new sensations. It is a form of being invisible, but not quite in the sense that you have so far mastered. This is object control and mind control. If done successfully, you can find out things about objects and people that will be nothing short of incredible.

The beginner should start with an object that is made up of a single material. A piece of steel or copper is good, so is a crystal or a small piece of wood. With the object in front of you, close your eyes and sit quietly. Visualize the object in your mind's eye. While you do that, enlarge the object. Think of it as growing, gradually, into something as large as, say, a door. Then think of yourself as moving into the object, merging with it, so that you are invisible to others inside this huge piece of steel or copper.

Now you are psychically one with the object. What do you do now? Whatever you do, you absolutely must keep you senses alive. Find out what you can see, feel, hear, and smell. Is it cold or warm inside? What sensations do you feel?

The answers to these questions won't come immediately. They will, however, emerge after you have succeeded with the method several times. This is another instance when your initial failures should be overlooked. The stance to take is: if others have done it, so can I.

The next step in the assumption method is to use a plant or a tree. If no trees are available to you, try a leaf on a house plant. You may pick a leaf and bring it into your house, but this represents a problem. A picked leaf is a dying one. There is still some life force in it, but it is waning.

It's best to try the experiment on a plant that is totally alive and still growing. Repeat the experiment that you performed with the inanimate object. Visualize the plant becoming extremely large. Use your imagination and see yourself merging with it. Check out your sensations while merged with the plant; when you have conquered that part of the method, move on to animals and humans.

Getting an animal or a human to sit for you while you assume to merge may be a problem, but at this stage of the game you are proficient enough to visualize the entity without having the physical presence. You are going to visualize the person anyway with your eyes closed, so you merely have to visualize that he or she is standing before you.

Merging with another person psychically is somewhat tricky. You are going to assume a merger, and for best results that individual should have his back to you in your imagination. Visualize putting your hands on both sides of his head. In your mind's eye, think and see yourself removing his head and putting it over your own head.

With his head on your shoulders, try to see with his eyes, hear with his ears, think with his brain. Yours and his thoughts should merge. There now should be telepathic communications, with you planting thoughts into his brain without his being aware of where they came from.

In the beginning of this phase of your experiment you may get only slight impressions from you host. You may see something that will tell you where he is at the moment of your assumption. In all likelihood you will have nothing. But stay with it. Practice will make you a success.

LEVITATION AND INVISIBILITY

Here are some examples of others who have mastered this technique:

* College students have merged with their professors to find out what questions they intended to ask on examinations.
* People who work with machinery have merged with the machinery to find out what was wrong.

* Computer technicians who have mastered the assumption method have merged with their computers to locate the bugs in the devices   an   advantage that saved them scores of man-hours in their work.

* Veterinarians who are unable to diagnose an illness in an animal by normal means will enter the pets mind to discover what the problem is.

* Gardeners can merge with their flowers and vegetables to ensure a perfect crop.

LEVITATION AND INVISIBILITY

Thoughts produce energy, and energy makes you more visible. Stop thinking, remain motionless with eyes closed, and you become invisible...not in the literal sense of the word, but unnoticed.

CHAPTER FOUR
PRAYERS AND SPELLS FOR INVISIBILITY

Some people who practice invisibility find that it helps to do some conjuring to get them into the mood. This is not true of those who follow the path of Yoga. You can be highly religious or an atheist, it makes no difference at all. But with magic, faith is required. It does not matter which faith you follow, but if you are going to invoke or pray, you should believe in the Supreme Deity or else you are being hypocritical.

This is the first prayer:

"Scaeboles, Arbaron, Elohi, Elimigith, Herenobulcule, Methe, Timayal, Villaquiel, Teveni, Yevie, Ferete, Bacuhavba, Guvarin; through Him through Whom ye have empire and power over men, ye must accomplish this work so that I may go and remain invisible.

"O thou Almiras, Master of Invisibility, with thy Ministers Cheros, Maitor, Tangedem, Transidium, Suvantos, Abelaios, Bored, Belamith, Castumi, Dabuel; I conjure ye by Him who maketh Earth and Heaven to tremble, Who is seated upon the throne of His majesty, that this operation may be perfectly accomplished according to my will, so that at whatsoever time it may please me, I may be able to be invisible."

When you have said that prayer you may want to say another to help you conjure up the cloud that will make you invisible:

"Come to me, O shroud of darkness and of night, by the power of the name Yeheshuah, Yehovashah. Formulate about me, thou divine egg of the darkness of spirit. I conjure ye, O particles of astral darkness, that ye enfold me as a guard and shroud of utter silence and mystery.

"I conjure and invoke this shroud of concealment. I invoke ye and conjure ye. I evoke ye potently. I command and constrain ye. I compel ye to absolute, instant, and complete obedience, and that

35

without deception and delay. And I declare that with the divine Aid in this Operation I shall succeed, that the shroud shall conceal me alike from men and spirits, that it shall be under my control, ready to disperse and to re-form at my command."

Another prayer in the form of a verse:

"Gather, ye flakes of Astral light
To shroud my form in your substantial Night;
Clothe me, and hide me, but at my control,
Darken men's eyes, and blind their souls;
Gather, O gather, at my word divine,
For ye are the Watchers, my soul is the shrine."

Still another prayer which may help you achieve your success:

"O ye strong and mighty ones of the Sphere of Shabbathai, ye Aralim, I conjure ye by the mighty name of Yhvh Elohim, the divine ruler of Binah, and by the name of Tzaphqiel, your Archangel. Aid me with your power, in your office to place a veil between me and all things belonging to the outer and material world. Clothe me with a veil woven from that silent darkness which surrounds your abode of eternal rest in the Sphere of Shabbathai."

When the moment comes that you want to become visible again, you may say the following prayer:

"In the name of Yhvh Elohim, I invoke thee, who art clothed with the Sun, who standest upon the Moon, and art crowned with the crown of twelve stars. Aima Elohim, Shekinah, Who art Darkness illuminated by the Light divine, send me thine Archangel Tzaphqiel, and thy legions of Aralim, the mighty angels of the Sphere of Shabbathai, that I may disintegrate and scatter this shroud of darkness and of mystery, for its work is ended for the hour.

"I conjure Thee, O shroud of darkness and of Mystery, which has well served my purpose, that thou now depart unto thine ancient ways. But be ye, whether by word or will, or by this great invocation of your powers, ready to come quickly and forcibly to my behest, again to shroud me from the eyes of men. And now I

LEVITATION AND INVISIBILITY

say unto ye, depart in peace, with the blessing of God the Vast and Shrouded One, and be ye very ready to come when ye are called."

These conjurations may help you to concentrate; and they may not. If they distract you, then they won't work for you. In any event, they are here for your benefit if you need something extra to aid you in becoming invisible.

An interesting spell for invisibility was written up in *The Circle Network News* Winter 93/94, Vol.15: Number 4 by author: Mara Ravensong Bluewater. The spell is a tried and true recipe for an invisibility manifesting preparation. The spell is presented as a powder, to be strewn, burned, or carried; the herbs given could just as well be concocted into a potion, oil, or tincture.

INVISIBILITY POWDER

At Dark Moon, in a mortar and pestle, grind together:

1 part Fern leaf, dried
1 part Poppy seeds Add:
2 parts Slippery Elm powder 1 part Myrrh
1 part Marjoram, dried
3 parts Dillweed, fresh if possible

Grind all together, mixing well. Add 9 drops almond tincture (almond cooking extract is great.) with enough spring water to make everything barely moist, and mix in well.

Place in a ceramic bowl, spreading as thinly as possible, and dry the mixture over low heat, stirring it occasionally, until it seems lightly browned. Pour back into mortar, and grind again, enchanting:

"Things Seen, and Things Not Seen: Let me walk here in between"

When finely powdered, store in a clear glass container. It will keep its power for years. Sprinkle, just a little bit, on yourself, objects, or in a place to be made invisible.

Another old herbal method of inducing invisibility involved using the poisonous Christmas rose. The plant was believed to serve in numerous powerful spells, including one that could ensure invisibility.

On the night of the new moon those wishing to become invisible must first bath themselves with rose water. Afterwards you must sit quietly and envision yourself to be as dark as the night of the new moon. At least 15 minutes of this mental activity must take place before any attempt at invisibility is made. At this point you must take the Christmas rose and tear it apart. As you take the plant apart, say with each piece, ***"these are my feet, these are my legs, this is my torso, these are my arms, these are my shoulders, this is my head."***

After completely tearing the plant into ten pieces then say out loud to the open sky: "As each piece of this plant disappears into the dark of the new moon, so will each piece of my body. With that, throw each piece, one at a time into the darkness. At the end of the ritual your body should be as dark as the night. As long as you do not make loud noises or attempt to draw unnecessary attention to yourself. You will remain unseen until the first light of the morning.

Another spell that has been handed down over the years involves taking a long cloak or coat and dipping it into the water of a pure running stream. You must do this everyday for twenty-eight days, starting on the first day of the new moon, and ending on the last day of the full moon.

You have to dip the coat thirteen times each day in order for the spell to work. On the beginning of the new month you can then wear the coat becoming as clear as the pure water. Unfortunately in modern times this spell probably won't work. The reason being is the difficulty finding a pure running stream of natural water. Any kind of pollution will negate the spell. Nor can you use filtered water, it must be clean, pure, natural water or the spell will not work.

CHAPTER FIVE
PROOF FOR THE REALITY OF INVISIBILITY

We've talked about how to become invisible, and we have dealt with the masters who know how to do it, but your must be asking yourself by now if the art is impossible. No one does it in real life. You have never come in contact with invisibility, nor do you know of anyone who has. Maybe so, but you can't convince Ernest Poindexter and Meredith Wright that they did not come in contact with an invisible man.

The date was September 1963 in Seattle, Washington. Ernest and Meredith at that time were nine years old. On that Saturday morning they were hitchhiking their way downtown to go to the movies.

A van stopped for them. The driver, an acquaintance of the family, said they were welcome to ride in the back, but that he had to make two stops before he got to the downtown area. Ernest and Meredith climbed in the back amid packages.

A few minutes later the driver stopped at a store where he had to make a delivery. He set the hand brake and put the transmission into reverse gear because he was parked on a hill.

While the driver was in the store, another vehicle pulled in behind the van and bumped it accidentally. The van started to roll. The hill was steep, and in no time at all the van was rolling at break-neck speed. Some parked cars were dead ahead. The children were panic-stricken. They didn't know what to do. There would be a terrible collision in a few seconds and there was nothing they could do about it.

Suddenly, the van lurched to the left and avoided the parked cars. A voice yelled out, "Don't be scared boys, just hang on tight. I'm going to apply the brakes."

The voice appeared to be coming from the drivers seat, but no one was there. Their eyes were glued to the steering wheel because it was turning by itself. Then the horn blew. They could see it being depressed as if by an unseen hand. Pedestrians scampered out of the way. Finally, at the bottom of the hill the van rolled to a stop. People came running over. The boys climbed down to the street. The van's driver hurried over to them. He said, "If you boys hadn't steered that truck you could have been killed."

Ernest said, "But we didn't steer it."

A pedestrian confirmed the boy's statement, saying that he saw the van and that no one was behind the wheel. Another onlooker said he saw the boys in the back, sitting on cartons, and that they were not behind the wheel.

The final confirmation came when the horn suddenly blew by itself in front of the astonished crowd. The two boys raced off. They wanted no part of the invisible man who came to their rescue.

Now that we know that invisibility does exist, it is not difficult to understand that at least one person in the Seattle area had accomplished the feat and had put it to good use.

HOW INVISIBILITY GAINED A KINGDOM

A shepherd named Gyges was caught in a violent storm while tending his flock. Then an earthquake ripped the ground asunder near where he was sitting. Gyges peered into the gap in the earth and saw to his surprise that it contained a hollow brazen horse. There were doors on each side of the horse. Gyges scampered down into the crevasse and opened one of the doors. Inside was an extremely large man who was obviously dead. He was nude except for a golden ring. Being a resourceful young man, Gyges took the ring and put it on his own finger.

This story, which comes from the works of Plato, continued with Gyges meeting with other shepherds during their monthly get-together. Their job was to prepare a report for the king concerning the state of their flocks. Gyges chatted away with his friends and played with the golden ring on his finger. He noticed that when he turned it so that the collet was inside his hand, the others in the group spoke of him as though he was no longer present. He realized in astonishment that the ring could make him invisible as long as he turned the collet to the inside of his hand.

Gyges saw great possibilities with the ring. He managed to get himself on the committee that was to present the monthly report to the king. Once inside the palace, he made himself invisible and hurried to the queen's chambers. He made love to the queen, who decided on the spot that Gyges was a better lover than the king. They then conspired to kill the king, which they did. And Gyges became the king of Lydia.

Plato let the story end there, but added a moral which said in essence to never trust an invisible man. Plato wrote: "Suppose that there were two such magic rings, and the just (man) put on one of them and the unjust man the other. No man can be imagined to be of such an iron nature that he would stand fast in justice. No man would keep his hands off what was not his own when he could safely take what he liked out of the market, or go into house and lie with anyone at his pleasure, or kill or release from prison whom he would, and in all respects be like a god among men. If you could imagine anyone obtaining this power of becoming invisible, and never doing any wrong or touching what was another's, he would be thought by the lookers-on to be a most wretched idiot. Although they would praise him to one another's faces, and keep up appearances with one another from fear that they, too, might suffer in injustice."

Plato was quite astute, although he did overlook the certainty, as one sage put it, "that God doth see both them and their knavery." Still, the philosopher's point is well taken. There is an ethical problem with invisibility, more so if one came upon a magic ring that could do the job. Fortunately, magic rings are few and far between.

A Chinese alchemist was wary of invisibility, saying that the techniques "are not to be used heedlessly, such as for example to produce outbursts of amazement when employed without reason in company. They may be used only in dire necessity against military reversals and dangerous crises, for in that way no harm will be incurred."

The Arab mystics and alchemists agree. They insist that invisibility should be used only on the battlefield and during a reversal of fortune. We must remember that these are ancient beliefs and that in today's world one cannot become invisible if one has an evil intent. That should have been clear even four centuries ago when two Spaniards wanted to kill the Prince of Orange. They assumed that they could do something similar to what Gyges did to gain the kingdom. The method they used has been lost, but we do know that apparently only one of them could become invisible, and only if he took all of his clothes off.

The date was March 18, 1582. The Spaniard who agreed to make himself invisible failed to look into a mirror to see if the experiment was successful. Instead, he walked naked to the palace. A guard let him pass. The Spaniard thought he was truly invisible because the guard gave no hint that he saw him. Actually he kept the naked man in view at all times, and when it appeared that the odd-looking stranger was intent on harming the prince, he was stopped. For his effort, the Spaniard was flogged soundly.

It is apparent that the ancients were well aware of the consequences of invisibility. Human's are susceptible to the lust of power and control. Invisibility can turn even the humblest man away from what is right.

LEVITATION AND INVISIBILITY

THE RING OF GYGES

Tradition has handed down through the ages the method of making the Ring of Gyges. For most however, to do so would mean Herculean feats of legerdemain.

The first step says to use fixed mercury. This is an alchemical term, and that refers to the Mercury of the Wise. Simply put, the Mercury of the Wise is the material that goes into the cloud you conjure up to make yourself invisible. Would it be even possible to shape this ethereal material into a solid ring?

The next step is even more difficult: You are to engrave the words "Jesus, passant par le milieu d'eux s'en allait" on the ring. The translation is that Jesus made himself invisible when he walked among the Pharisees. We are not told how to engrave something on a cloud.

The ring must be set with a small stone found in the lapwing's nest. This is called Quiritia. Finding a lapwing bird may not be easy.

There are also certain mystifications that come from the rather vulgar grimoires. Since we are not likely to make such a ring, why bother? There are other ridiculous methods of becoming invisible, such as weaving the hairs from the head of a hyena. Those hairs are so short that it would be close to impossible to weave them.

We think our methods of making yourself invisible are much more sensible, however you should be aware of the more far-fetched methods as they may well have worked for someone else in the past.

THE STRANGE CASE OF MADAME BLAVATSKY

Madame Blavatsky was a Russian occultist who was said to have codified secret traditional truths into two basic textbooks, *Isis Unveiled*, and ***The Secret Doctrine***. She established the Theosophical Society in 1875 with a membership of 15. Today there are 1500 branches throughout the world, with several hundred thousand members. Madame Blavatsky said that she was guided into setting up the society by a spirit, and that her acute psychic powers came from an invisible band of Tibetan "masters of wisdom."

Madame Blavatsky also claimed she had the power of invisibility. A man called Colonel Olcott wrote an eyewitness account of one incident which indicates that the woman was truly capable of this feat. Olcott wrote:

"Her house in Philadelphia was built on the local plan, with a front building and a wing at the back which contained the dining-room below and sitting or bedroom above. Madame Blavatsky's bedroom was the front room on the first floor of the main building; at the turn of the staircase was the sitting room, and from its open door one could look straight along the passage into her room if the door was open. Madame Blavatsky had been sitting in the former apartment conversing with me, but left to get something from her bedroom. I saw her mount the few steps to her floor, enter her room, and leave the door open. Time passed, but she did not return. I waited, and waited. Fearing that she might have fainted, I called her name. There was no reply, so now, being a little anxious, and knowing that she could not be engaged privately, since the door had not been closed. I went in, called again, and looked under the bed. She was not there. I looked in her closet. She was not visible anywhere. She had vanished, without the chance of having walked out in the normal way, for, save the door giving upon the landing, there was no other means of exit; the room was a cul de sac.

"I was a cool one about phenomena after my long course of experiences, but this puzzled and worried me. I went back to the sitting room, lit a pipe, and tried to puzzle out the mystery. This was in 1875, many years before the Salpetriere school's experiments in hypnotism had been vulgarized, so it never occurred to me that I was the subject of a neat experiment in mental suggestion, and that Madame Blavatsky had simply inhibited my organs of sight from perceiving her presence, perhaps within two paces of me in the room. After a while she calmly came out of her room into the passage and returned to the sitting room to me. When I asked her where she had been, she laughed and said she had some occult business to attend to, and had made herself invisible. But how, she could not explain."

INVISIBILITY THROUGH HYPNOTISM

The subject was an 18 year old girl named Elsie B. As reported by a doctor named Binet, the servant girl was placed in a deep hypnotic trance. The hypnotist told her: "When you awaken you will no longer see me. I shall have gone."

She woke, and just as predicted, she did not notice the hypnotist. She looked for him, even though he was sitting directly in front of her. He shouted at her but she did not hear him. He stuck pins into her flesh, but she did not feel the pain. "As far as she was concerned," the hypnotist said, "I had ceased to exist, and all the acoustic, visual, tactile, and other impressions emanating from myself did not make the slightest impression upon her; she ignored them all . . . Wishing to see, on account of its medical-legal bearing, whether a serious offense might be committed under cover of hypnosis, I roughly raised her dress and skirt. Although naturally very modest, she allowed this without a blush. A moment later, though, she was blushing a very great deal."

LEVITATION AND INVISIBILITY

That was because the hypnotist suggested to her that she would remember that incidents that, a moment before, she did not even seem to be aware of. She did remember, yet she was altogether unable to believe that she had allowed herself to be exposed, and, when queried, reported that she remembered the incident as if it took place in a dream.

The demonstration harkens back to ancient times when people were struck blind without any apparent damage to the eyes. Today the condition is called hysteria or conversion neurosis, and people are rarely "struck blind" because faith is the essential factor in the disease, and faith is the essential factor in the cure.

Peter B.C. Fenwick a London psychiatrist and neurophysiologist, conducted research on a woman known as Ruth because of her ability to see apparitions that looked as real to her as living persons did. These apparitions did not have the insubstantial quality of ghosts or dreams. Ruth said they obstructed her view of things just as real people would.

Fenwick fitted Ruth with electrodes on her scalp. The electrodes showed through an oscilloscope, that electrical waves from the vision center of Ruth's brain were stimulated every time she created one of her apparitions. To Ruth's brain, her mind created apparitions that were as real as the electrodes on her head.

When asked how she made an apparition, Ruth replied: "I stop paying attention to everything around me. I decide whose apparition I want to make. I remember what the person looks like, as most people do with their eyes closed, except my eyes are open. And I produce the person."

Tests showed that when Ruth was seeing and hearing an apparition, her brain reacted as it would when perceiving a live person. Ruth's ability shows that the brain can be instructed to "see" what is not there, and to "not see" what is there.

In his book **The Holographic Universe**, science writer Michael Talbot describes an incident in which a man is hypnotized in a room full of people including his teenage daughter, and is given the post-hypnotic suggestion that, upon awakening, his daughter will be invisible to him. When bought out of his trance, not only could he apparently not see the giggling girl standing in front of him, but, when the hypnotist stood behind her and held a watch against her back, he was able to read the inscription on it as if he was looking right through her body. Talbot, who actually spoke to the man, was unable to explain the incident, but suggested that perhaps he was obtaining the information via telepathy.

Hypnotism, which has gone by many names, has been used throughout the ages to control the minds of others. History has shown that there are those who seem to have an innate ability to influence others. Some call this charisma, but in essence, it is really the mastery of controlling the minds of others. Again, the desire for power is an evil influence for this ability.

With the proper types of practice, a person can influence the minds of those around him to literally "not see" you. This is why learning to control your own thoughts is so important. In order to control the minds of those you want to be invisible to, you must be able to control your own mind. A noisy, energetic mind will allow your image to "bleed" over into other minds. As long as your image remains in the brains of those you are trying to disappear from, invisibility will be impossible.

SPONTANEOUS INVISIBILITY

Researcher Donna Higbee is a hypnotherapist in Santa Barbara, California. Higbee runs a support group for people who believe that they have experienced some form of encounter and/or abduction by alien entities. The meetings offer a totally open and safe space for a dialogue regarding personal experiences, personal beliefs, and the implications of what such encounters might mean in a larger sense for this planet.

Donna was not surprised when a woman asked to speak about something that she didn't know how to deal with or understand. After hearing the story, Higbee at first thought there was the possibility that this individual was highly imaginative. However, when a second person some time later spoke of the same thing, Donna Higbee decided to look into the situation further.

Vera (pseudonym), the first woman, had a very unusual story: Vera had driven her car to the post office to get stamps. She walked in and joined the line, taking the end position. Soon thereafter a man walked in and asked the man directly in front of Vera if this was the end of the line. The man ahead of Vera answered that he was indeed the end of the line, wherein Vera spoke up and said she was the end of the line. No one looked at Vera or acknowledged that she had spoken and. in fact she was almost stepped on as the second man took up the end position in line.

Vera thought to herself how rude these people were and moved slightly to the side of the line, so as not to be jostled; she continued moving up with other people. When her time came to go to the counter to be helped, she walked up and stated her business and quite to her amazement, the man behind her walked right up and did the same. The postal clerk never acknowledged Vera but began assisting the man. Vera announced loudly that she was there first, but no one paid the slightest attention to her. Getting very upset by this time with what she considered extreme rudeness, she just walked out of the post office and went home. A number of days later, she was attempting to get some assistance in a store and no one would help her or even acknowledge that she was present. It seemed as if she was invisible to people around her and also couldn't be heard when she spoke. She had no idea what was happening, but she certainly wasn't pleased about it.

When a second person came to Higbee with a story that seemed to involve invisibility, she began to take this a little more seriously. In brief, this woman was sitting on the sofa, letting her mind wander as she stared at the wall. The wall seemed to take on a less- than- solid form and she was fascinated with it. When she finally came out of her reverie, she was astonished to find her husband searching the house for her and she certainly had not been there. Again, although she was physically present, the woman seemed to be unseen by another person. She had become invisible.

At his point, Higbee decided to check with a number of other researchers and see if anyone else had ever heard of such a report. She was surprised to find that a number of other researchers had in just the past year or so either heard of this, or knew someone directly who had experienced something akin to spontaneous invisibility.

In every case Higbee researched, the person was physically still present, although unable to be seen or heard. From the point of view of the invisible person, the world

looks normal and they have no idea that they cannot be seen or heard by people around them.

Donna Higbee spoke with two individuals in different towns in Texas who reported invisibility experiences. One woman went through a cafeteria line and when she approached the cashier, the cashier couldn't see her. It was only when the woman began to get upset that the cashier suddenly saw her standing there.

Another woman who had similar experiences wanted to conduct a little experiment. After having been ignored at a movie theater ticket window, she proceeded to walk in and out of the theater past the ticket person several times. No one ever indicated that they could see her. Then to be absolutely certain, she entered the lobby of the men's room to see if she could get stares. No one even looked her way.

Jean in Tucson, Arizona, wrote Higbee of her experiences. She has had them occur in the library when she attempted to check out books and in clothing stores. "I've had this happen in stores, in restaurants, and many places. I remember joking to a friend of mine one time that I felt like I could walk into a bank, help myself to a pile of bills and no one would ever see me because I was invisible. There is no physical reason why I should be. I'm taller than average for my sex and age group (I'm fifty-five years old and 5'9"), referred to as good-looking, and I've always worn my hair red. You wouldn't think a tall woman with red hair, high heels in a purple dress and dangle earrings would be invisible, would you?"

Then there is the story from thirty-seven year old Peter in Gloucestershire, England, who was at a private party in 1987. He walked upstairs to use the bathroom and was followed by a woman who also wanted to use the bathroom. The woman motioned for him to go first and she stood outside the door to wait her turn. Peter used the bathroom, opened the door and walked out into the hallway, closing the door behind him. He went on down the stairs and walked over to some friends and started talking to them. They all ignored him completely. He though they were playing a joke on him, so he walked away and found his girlfriend and asked her for a cigarette. She, too, acted like she didn't see or hear him.

Peter was getting angry by this time and thought the joke had gone too far. He decided to walk back upstairs and catch the woman coming out of the bathroom and ask her for a cigarette. "...I walked back up the stairs and, on reaching the bathroom landing, I came across the girl again who was standing outside the bathroom door, clearly still waiting for me to come out. When she saw me, her face dropped in surprise for clearly she thought that I was still in the bathroom." Peter returned to the party downstairs and everything was normal again and he was able to be seen and heard. When he questioned his friends and girlfriend as to why they had ignored him, they all swore that they had never seen or heard him. Obviously the woman upstairs had not seen him come out of the bathroom and go downstairs.

Jannise of Minneapolis, Minnesota has had a number of invisibility experiences throughout her life. As a teenager, she fell in with a group of friends who decided to see if they could actually steal something from a department store and not get caught. As luck would have it, the entire group was caught and taken into custody, including Jannise. They were taken to the police station and one by one were questioned, except for Jannise.

Although she was standing right there, no one paid the slightest attention to her; not the police, the guards, or the office personnel. She finally just got up and walked out of the police station without ever being questioned or anyone attempting to stop her. When she later talked with her friends about what happened in the police station, "...they didn't even recall me being taken into custody at the department store. Yet I rode in the police car with everyone else, and they thought I was still at the store." No one had seen her from the moment the police had arrived on the scene in the store until some time after she had walked out of the police station unhindered.

LEVITATION AND INVISIBILITY

Higbee wonders if there is any kind of correlation between those individuals who feel they have been aboard an alien craft, and those who are experiencing this invisibility phenomenon. It would be interesting to learn if, in passing through the force field of a craft, the abductee's own vibrational frequency is somehow altered or raised. Reported UFOs seem to have the ability to appear and disappear at will and might have a force field that alters vibrational frequency and allows for spontaneous invisibility.

INVISIBLE BEINGS

Caroline Cory, in her article *Organization of Intelligent Beings on Earth*, writes that spirit or physical beings from other systems do not need to be visible and materialize in order to co-exist with you on Earth. In fact, there are a great number of intelligent beings currently present on Earth that are entirely unnoticed by you. Physical beings are evolutionary, which means they must incarnate in a physical apparatus (not necessarily human) in order to evolve consciously. While their physical appearance may be relatively complete, their brain capacity and mind expansion continue to advance exponentially.

Your planet is one of the many worlds which are inhabited by physical beings. You are beginning to awaken to their existence and will soon openly embrace your common galactic heritage. In terms of consciousness evolution, humans are the juveniles of material creation but are moving rapidly to the enlightened attainments of their neighboring planets. A myriad of non-human physical beings from other systems are currently on Earth but remain invisible due to the time/space or frequency layer they exist in. They are also able to manipulate their energy field through de-particularization and travel through your system without being perceived. Their role and function vary from planetary scientific observation and research, to the teaching of spiritual emancipation.

Visible and invisible physical beings currently on Earth can be categorized as follows:

HUMAN BEINGS: These are the humans born on Earth who are, of course, physical and visible. Humans typically do not recall their pre-natal agreement and must begin their life on Earth. They will normally incarnate in a few and up to thousands of physical embodiments until they realize their unlimited divine self and master their creative powers and mind potential. They are then able to move to more evolved worlds and carry on with their soul journey.

LEVITATION AND INVISIBILITY

VISIBLE NON-HUMAN BEINGS: These beings appear as normal humans, however their ancestry or soul lineage as well as their genetic encoding stem from another evolved star or planetary system . They incarnate as humans and awaken gradually to their true non-human identity. They are normally unaware of their role or mission until they remember their pre-natal agreement while in the flesh. In very rare instances, these beings may ?walk-in? fully aware of their Earthly contract. These unique individuals normally work in unison with other divine entities for your species? evolution and transmutation to the next order of existence.

INVISIBLE PHYSICAL BEINGS: These beings have evolved further than humans and are in physical form. They have developed advanced skills in telekinesis, technology and science. However, because they exist in a different time / space continuum and vibrate at a different wavelength, they cannot be perceived by humans. Occasional breaches in the fabric of the time / space arrangement allow humans to perceive and interact with these beings. Sightings of aliens, reptilians and the like fit in this category of non-visible physical beings.

The CELESTIAL BEINGS organization on Earth consists of thousands upon thousands of invisible spirit beings, forces and agencies ministering to the growth and well-being of your planet. They are mostly of the seraphic order and act as messengers, guides, transport and death agents. They function under the supervision of planetary supervisors and controllers.

The divine members of these celestial governments are the Energy Controllers of all material worlds. They insure proper ministry of the evolutionary species and maintain the harmonic balance of the planet with its neighboring worlds. Spirit beings are created but they are not evolutionary because they do not require embodiment in the physical in order to attain complete self-realization. Their mind expansion happens through their very function and purpose.

Celestial Beings on your planet can be categorized as follows:

SPIRIT BEINGS: They vibrate at an extremely high rate and are invisible to humans. All Spirit entities, angels, elementals, power controllers, architects, translators and guides fit in this category. They utilize the cosmic forces available to them to assist human existence. They can make themselves temporarily visible to humans in order to deliver a message or perform a specific task. They work under the supervision and control of the Divine Planetary Supervisor and the Celestial Government.

PHYSICAL DIVINE BEINGS: These beings are visible to humans. Superhuman physical beings are those who incarnate with the knowledge of their Creator-Energy lineage, for the purpose of teaching it to others or for other planetary purpose. They may come in with the superhuman gift as a grown adult totally aware of whom they are. However, due to their important energetic collapse at the time of physical emergence, they will typically remember their divine heritage as they gradually grow up in the form of a normal human being. Their original state of being is that of Light and pure Creator Energy and they are the direct incarnation of the Creator-Father / the Creator-Source. They carry both a human and a unique sacred encoding which remains undetected by human awareness. They utilize their special encoding to access divine information while they outwardly function as a normal human in the flesh.

Communication happens consciously through the use of language and spontaneously though thought. When you think, you emit a frequency wave equivalent to the emotions attached to the meaning of your words and intent. Contrary to common belief, Thought exists in a physical medium and has an actual measurable wavelength. Those beings that function in that frequency range, may be invisible to you, but are very much real, able to ?read? your thoughts and project theirs back onto you.

Therefore you are communicating spontaneously, through your thoughts, with an invisible world and beings, physical or non-physical, human or non-human. This naturally occurring phenomenon must not, however, be confused with mind control which is the deliberate alteration of the thoughts of another. You can most certainly be influenced by the invisible beings? thoughts, just as you can be influenced by your visible friends, but it always remains your choice to become controlled entirely by the thoughts and intention of another.

THE INVISIBLE JINN

Throughout history man has always had a deep attraction for the supernatural and the unseen. The existence of a world parallel to our own has always fascinated people. This world is commonly referred to as the spirit world, and almost every set of people have some concept of one. With some people, these spirits are no more than the souls of dead people-or ghosts. With others, spirits are either the forces of good or the forces of evil - both battling against one another to gain influence over humanity.

One group of invisible beings are the Jinn. They are beings created with free will and living on Earth in a world parallel to mankind. The Arabic word Jinn is from the verb 'Janna' which means to hide or conceal. Thus, they are physically invisible from man as their description suggests. This invisibility is one of the reasons why some people have denied their existence.

LEVITATION AND INVISIBILITY

Jinn are conscious beings charged with Divine obligations. The word jinn literally means something hidden or veiled from sight. As mentioned earlier, jinns are a species of invisible beings. A short Qur'anic chapter is named for them, and in it we learn that a band of jinn listened to Prophet Muhammad, upon him be peace and blessings, and some became believers: Say:

"It has been revealed to me that a company of the jinn gave ear, and they said: 'We have heard a wonderful Qur'an, which guides to righteousness, so we believe in it and we shall not join (in belief and worship) any (Gods) with our Allah. And (we believe) that He-exalted be the glory of our Allah-has taken neither wife nor son .... Among us there are righteous folk and among us there are far from that. We are sects having different rules.," (72:1-2, 11) From this, we understand that jinn are conscious beings charged with Divine obligations.

Recent discoveries in biology make it clear that Allah created beings particular to each realm in the universe. Jinn might have been created while the Earth was still a body of some sort of fire. They were created before Adam and Eve, and were responsible for cultivating and improving the world. Although Allah later superseded them with us, He did not exempt them from religious obligations.

The Qur'an states that jinn are created from smokeless fire (55:15). In another verse, it clarifies that this fire is scorching and penetrates as deep as the inner part of the body (15:27). In modern terms, we may say that humans are carbon-based or water-based, jinns plasma-based.

Like angels, jinn move extremely fast and are not bound by the time and space constraints within which we normally move. However, since the spirit is more active and faster than jinn, a person who lives at the level of the spirit's life and who can transcend what we know as limits of matter and the confines of time and space, can be quicker and more active than them. For example, the Qur'an relates that when Prophet Solomon asked those around him who could bring the throne of the Queen of Saba' (Yemen), one jinn answered that he could bring it before the meeting ended and Prophet Solomon stood up. However, a man with a special knowledge from Allah replied: "I can bring it to you quicker than the blink of an eye," and he did so (27:38-40).

Power and strength are not limited to the physical world, nor are they proportional to bodily size. We see that immaterial things are far more powerful than huge physical entities. For example, our memory is far more spacious and comprehensive than a large room. Our hands can touch a very near object, but our eyes can travel long distances in an instant, and our imagination can transcend time and space all at once. Winds can uproot trees and demolish large buildings. A young, thin plant shoot can split rocks and reach the sunlight. The power of energy, whose existence is known through its effect, is apparent to everybody. All of this shows that something's power is not proportional to its physical size; rather the immaterial world dominates the physical world, and immaterial entities are far more powerful than material ones.

Angels and jinn can assume a form and appear in this world in the shape of any being. Here, we observe movement from the visible to the invisible: water evaporates disappears into the atmosphere, solid matter becomes a liquid or a gas (steam), and matter becomes energy (nuclear fission). Likewise, we observe movement from the invisible to the visible: gases become fluids, evaporated water becomes rain (as well as snow or hail), and energy becomes matter. Similarly, intangible thoughts and meanings in our minds can appear in the tangible form of letters and words in essays and books.

In an analogous way, such invisible beings as angels, jinn, and other spirit entities are clothed in some material substance, such as air or ether, and then become visible. According to Imam Shibli, if Allah wills, He allows them to assume a form when they utter any of His Names, for this functions like a key or a visa enabling them to assume a form and become visible in this world. If they try to do so without Allah permission, by relying on their own abilities, they are torn into pieces and perish.

We read in Qur'an 19:17 that the spirit Allah sent to Mary (the mother of Jesus), and whom Muslim scholars say is the Archangel Gabriel, appeared before her as a man. When Gabriel came to Prophet Muhammad, upon him be peace and blessings, with Revelation or Allah Messages, he rarely appeared in his original form. Rather, he usually came as a warrior, a traveler, or a Companion named Dihya. For example, he came as a warrior on horseback following the end of the Battle of the Trench and told the Prophet, upon him be peace: "O Messenger of Allah, you have taken off your armor but we, the angels, have not yet done so. Allah orders you to march upon the Banu Qurayza." Once he came as a traveler dressed in white and, in order to instruct the Companions in religion, asked the Prophet such questions as: What is belief? What is Islam? What is ihsan (excellence or perfection of virtue)? When is the Day of Judgment?

Like angels and jinn, Satan (who belongs to the jinn) also can appear in different forms. It is narrated that before the Battle of Badr, he appeared to the leaders of the Quraysh as an old man from Najd and gave them some advice. Likewise, a Companion guarding the spoils of war caught a disguised Satan trying to steal some of the booty (most probably to lead other Companions to suspect that Companion). He entreated the Companion to release him, which he did-twice. On the third time, the Companion tried to take him to Allah Messenger. But Satan appealed: "Release me, and I will tell you how you can secure yourself against me." The Companion asked what that was, and Satan replied that it was the Verse of the Throne (2:255). When informed of the event, Allah's Messenger, upon him be peace and blessings, commented: "That wicked one is a liar, but on that occasion he told the truth."

The Qur'an relates that a group of jinn listened to Allah Messenger reciting the Qur'an and, when they returned to their people, said: "O people! Surely we listened to a Book that has been revealed after Moses, affirms what precedes it, and guides to right and the Straight Path" (46:30). The sura continues with what they thought about what they had heard. There are also Traditions that tell us that the Messenger, upon him be peace and blessings, recited parts of the Qur'an and preached his Message to the jinn.

Jinn can also appear as snakes, scorpions, cattle, donkeys, birds, and other animals. When our Prophet, upon him be peace and blessings, took the oath of allegiance from them in the valley of Batn al-Nakhla, he wanted them to appear to his community either in their own form or in other agreeable forms, not in the forms of such harmful animals as dogs and scorpions. He warned his community: When you see any vermin in your house, tell it three times: "For Allah sake, leave this place," for it may be a friendly jinn. If it does not leave, it is not a jinn. If it is harmful, you may kill it.

The jinn who gave allegiance to Allah Messenger promised him: "If your community recites the basmala (In the Name of Allah, the All-Merciful, the All-Compassionate) before anything they do and cover their dishes, we will not touch their food or their drink." Another Tradition says: [When you have relieved yourselves] do not clean yourselves with bones and dried pieces of dung, for they are among the foods of your jinn brothers.

Some people have an innate ability to go into trance and contact beings from the invisible realms of existence. However, it should not be forgotten that whether these are angels or jinn, invisible beings have their own conditions of life and are bound to certain limits and principles. For this reason, one who gets in touch with jinn should be careful, for one may easily fall under their influence and become their plaything.

Some assert that the Mirza Ghulam Ahmad (1839-1908) of Qadiyan (India), fell victim to such tricks of jinn. He attempted to serve Islam by struggling against Hindu Yogism through the way of Fakirism, but evil spirits got control of him. First they whispered to him that he was a reviver (of religion), then that he was the Mahdi (Messiah), and when he was finally under their influence and control, told him to proclaim that he was an incarnation of Allah.

Sins and being unclean invite the influence of evil spirits and unbelieving jinns. People of a susceptible nature, those who tend to be melancholy, and those who lead a dissipated and undisciplined life are their primary targets.

LEVITATION AND INVISIBILITY

Evil spirits usually reside in places for dumping garbage or other dirty places, public baths, and bathrooms.

Jinn can penetrate a body even deeper than X-rays. They can reach into a being's veins and the central points of the brain. They seem to be like lasers, which are used in everything from computers to nuclear weaponry, from medicine to communication and police investigations, and to removing obstructions in our veins and arteries. So, when we consider that Satan and all jinn are created from smokeless fire that penetrates deep into the body, like radiation or radioactive energy, we can understand the meaning of the Prophetic Tradition: Satan moves where the blood moves.

Jinn can harm the body and cause physical and psychological illnesses. It might be a good idea for medical authorities to consider whether jinn cause certain types of cancer, since cancer is an unordered and diseased growth in the body that we describe as a kind of cellular anarchy. Maybe some jinn have settled in that part of the body and are destroying its cellular structure.

Although science does not yet accept the existence of invisible beings and restricts itself to the material world, we think it is worth considering the possibility that evil spirits play some part in such mental illnesses as schizophrenia. We constantly hear of cases that those who suffer from mental illness, epilepsy, or even cancer recover by reciting certain prayers. Such cases are serious and significant, and should not be denied or dismissed by attributing them to "suggestion" or "auto-suggestion." When science breaks the thick shell in which it has confined itself and accepts the existence of the metaphysical realm and the influence of metaphysical forces, it practitioners will be able to remove many obstructions, make far greater advances, and make fewer mistakes.

Today, the doors to the metaphysical worlds are only slightly ajar. We are barely at the beginning of contact with jinn and devils. However, one day we will feel constrained to enter these worlds to solve many of their problems pertaining to this world.

The Qur'an states that Allah bestowed upon the House of Abraham the Scripture, Wisdom, and a mighty kingdom (4:54). This mighty kingdom manifested itself most brilliantly through the Prophets David and Solomon, upon them be peace.

Prophet Solomon ruled not only a part of humanity, but also jinn and devils, birds and winds: Allah subdued unto him devils, some of whom dove for pearls and did other work (21:82). Solomon had armies of jinn and birds, and he employed jinn in many jobs: They made for him what he willed: synagogues, fortresses, basins like wells and boilers built into the ground (34:13); and Wind was also subdued to him; its morning course was a month's journey and the evening course also a month's journey (34:12). As pointed out earlier, the throne of the Queen of Saba' was carried from Yemen to Jerusalem in the twinkling of an eye (27:40).

The verses relating to Solomon's kingdom point to the final limit of humanity's use of jinn and devils. These also suggest that a day will come when we can use them in many jobs, especially in communication. It is quite probable that they also will be employed in security affairs, mining and metal-work, even in space studies and historical research. Since jinn can live about 1,000 years, they may be useful in establishing historical facts.

EXTRATERRESTRIAL OR EXTRADIMENTIONAL?

Gordon Creighton, in his ground-breaking article *The True Nature Of UFO Entities*, lists ten chief characteristics of the jinns.

1. In the normal state they are not visible to ordinary human sight.

2. They are, however, capable of materializing and appearing in the physical world. And they can alternately make themselves visible or invisible at will.

3. They can change shape, and appear in any sort of guise, large or small.

4. They are able also to appear in the guise of animals.

5. They are inveterate liars and deceivers, and delight in bamboozling and misleading mankind with all manner of nonsense.

6. They are addicted to the abduction or kidnapping of humans.

7. They delight in tempting humans into sexual intercourse and liaisons with them.

8. The jinns are wont to snatch up humans and teleport or transport them, setting them down again - if indeed they ever do set them down again - miles away from where they were picked up, and all this is the "twinkling of an eye".

9. The Arabian tradition asserts that, throughout all known history, there have been a few particular human beings who, through some strange favour, have "been in league with the jinns or had pact with the jinns – to such a degree that the jinns have endowed them with what we regard as "preternatural powers."

10. Along with all these displays of prowess by the jinns there goes, finally, a tremendous telepathic power and the ability to "CAST A GLAMOUR" over their human victims.

LEVITATION AND INVISIBILITY

The Dictionary of Islam by Thomas Patrick Hughes states: "They become invisible at please (by a rapid extension or rarefaction of the particles which compose them), or suddenly disappear in the earth or air, or through a solid wall." Particles in plasma, through magnetic and electric forces, can increase their inter-particle distance to decrease the density of the plasma. The inter-particle distance in collisionless plasma is so large that objects of collisionless plasma can easily pass through each other.

All of these characteristics associated with the jinn are consistent with plasma life forms. Some writers have already argued that jinns are in fact plasma life forms, for example, Dr Ibrahim B Syed, a Clinical Professor of Medicine at the University of Louisville, School of Medicine.

We should note that the concept of plasma is a relatively modern one. The term "plasma" was coined by Irving Langmuir around 1929 and modern plasma physics only began in the twentieth century. A thousand years ago the concept of plasma did not exist. But the term "smokeless fire" captures rather nicely the image of a plasma. If we had fluorescent lamps and neon signs (which are composed of plasma) a thousand years ago, they would probably be described as "smokeless fire" or "fire without smoke".

Jinns cannot see human beings clearly but only as blurred images. However, just like humans, the perceptual ranges of some jinns may be wider giving them intermittent access to the human world (just as some humans have intermittent access to the jinn world). It will not be surprising if these jinns are considered "psychic" in their own world - being the few who are able to communicate with a strange species called "humans". The majority of jinns would probably consider humans as ghosts living in a parallel Earth.

Like human beings, jinns are entrusted with responsibilities (careers, family life, etc.). We are told that many jinns accepted the mission and message of the Holy Prophet when they heard the Holy Qur'an read by the Prophet while performing "Fajr salaah" in Ukaz. It is therefore believed that jinns, just like humans, congregate into different religions and come together in different groups, sects and cults such as Muslims, Christians, Jews and even presumably atheists. They would have their own mosques, churches and temples - as reported by some persons who have had near-death experiences. In other words, jinns operate in societies, communities and within political systems and are startlingly similar to humans. Their plasma-based civilization has probably a longer history than ours.

Jinns are believed to be more numerous than humans on Earth. The author of Lawaami al-Anwaar al-Bahiya mentions a hadith as follows: "The jinn have children in the same way that the sons of Adam have children, but theirs are more in number." Hughes' Dictionary of Islam states that the jinn "propagate their species, sometimes in conjunction with human beings; in which latter case, the offspring partakes of the nature of both parents." This suggests the existence of jinn-human hybrids. A jinn-human hybrid can effectively live in two different "universes" and prevent the extermination of personal identity through the death of any one body.

For example, it is conceivable that the jinn component could separate itself from the human carbon and water-based body on the death of the latter and then propagate itself and its identity (which has now been enriched by the human experiences) through another human in a type of reincarnation. The jinn component could also separate itself when the human component is sleeping to visit other entities at its own energy level. In a sense, therefore, the genie leaves the bottle every time the hybrid sleeps and permanently on death.

Just like humans, individual jinns also die and are therefore not immortal. However, the personal identity of a human-jinn hybrid can conceivably be sustained for a long time by transferring the information relating to the personal identity or the "autobiographical memory" of the hybrid back and forth between the human and jinn components whose life spans are slightly out-of-phase. This is analogous to transferring a computer file from the hard drive in your computer to an external hard drive and vice-versa. But there is a missing piece - the receiving human being must have a way to generate a new bioplasma body for the older jinn to transfer the autobiographical memory of the deceased human-jinn hybrid. The new human-jinn hybrid can then pass on the memories to the next hybrid, and the cycles of existence repeat.

The human's carbon-based body has a brain that is composed of billions of neurons and even larger number of neural networks that can encode vast amounts of information. On the other hand, in the jinn's bioplasma body, we can imagine sophisticated holographic memory systems using plasma liquid crystal. A digital holographic system has been built by scientists at Stanford University and sophisticated real-time liquid crystal holographic memory systems have been created by Penn State engineers.

Normally, the jinn are invisible to human eyes. However, under certain circumstances, the jinn can assume a form and appear in this world in the shape of any type of being.

CHAPTER SIX
HOW UFOs BECOME INVISIBLE

Many years ago, Alexander Graham Bell the inventor of the telephone, wrote an article for a scientific magazine explaining how it was possible for metal to disappear. He wrote: "If you place a rod in the ground and electrically vibrated this rod, at first you would feel its oscillation. If it were vibrating a little faster you would expert to hear a hum coming from the shaft. Should it be heightened further, it would eventually become magnetic. By adding more resonance to the rod, it would begin to produce electrical energies. Further increasing the rod's intensity, would then cause its to become warm, proceeding onward through the temperature range, revealing colors associated with heat; red, orange, yellow, blue, violet, and so on.

"Then as the vibrations are augmented, it enters the radio spectrum, producing radio waves. Beyond that, it would enter the chemical range in the forty-eighth or forty-ninth octave. Still increasing the intensity of oscillation, it will begin to produce light around the fiftieth octave. A little higher up it goes into the realm of x-rays. Here, it would become dangerous to touch, or to be too near the rod.

"More rapid oscillations cause the rod to give off gamma rays which are very dangerous to the human form. Then proceeding on up higher in the spectrum, the so- called cosmic rays begin to make their presence known. So from a few vibrations a second, to countless millions (numbers with seventeen or eighteen decimals) the rod continues to blur as it vibrates with increasing intensity. Eventually, it will become invisible, and then who knows where it would go from there."

It's quite possible that UFOs, which appear suddenly in the sky, and just as suddenly disappear, operate on Bell's theory of extreme vibration. Of course, the occupants of the spacecraft must be capable of withstanding the enormous pressure, a feat which would kill humans.

A startling photo taken by an unsuspecting visitor at high noon at the foot of Starr Hill in Warminster, U.K., depicts an object - a dark ominous shape - which the human eye was unable to detect. There on two different frames of 35mm film taken by John Wright was a giant black globe the likes of which were not observed. A check of the equipment showed no defect. When asked if he had noticed anything unusual at the time, Wright states he was aware only of the deathly silent and brooding atmosphere of his surroundings.

In his book, *Flying Saucers on the Attack* (Citadel Press), Harold T. Wilkins writes that in both London and NY, attempts were made as far back as the 30's, to produce invisibility by warping light rays in an electromagnetic field. In 1934 in London, there was demonstrated in a public hall apparatus which was perhaps suggested by the fantasy of the late H.G. Wells' "The Invisible Man."

A young scientist, wearing what he called an Electro-Helmet and a special Mantle, went into a cabinet open at the front before a brilliantly lit stage. He then with both hands, touched contact gloves which were over his head.

An electric current was switched on and the man's body gradually vanished from feet to head. One could step up and touch him but could not see him. Nor did the camera reveal the secret, for it depicted only what the eye saw.

The inventor refused to reveal his secret which he said was the work of many years of experiments. All one could see was the development of a cone of light such as might be projected between the two poles of a powerful transmitter. This cone persisted even when the man could not be seen.

The inventor had succeeded in doing on stage in public what a dematerializing apparition is alleged to do in a haunted house. Whether he developed the powers of some new or previously discovered ray and created an opaque screen is hard to say. However, the inventor may have been the first to stumble upon the science that years later would be developed for the infamous "Philadelphia Experiment."

INVISIBLE FLYING OBJECTS

Catching a glimpse of a UFO is often a rare experience. If everyone could see UFOs darting about in our air space, there would be no doubts that UFOs exist. UFOs are classified as "phenomena" because sightings are rare (except in UFO hotspots) and there are so few witnesses. Many people have never seen a UFO and some people live their entire lives without ever seeing one. The rarity of observing UFOs, the lack of public acknowledgement that UFOs exist, government debunking and ridicule of witnesses who do come forward, and various human belief systems divide world populations into those who believe UFOs exist, those who do not and the "undecided."

Some researchers theorize that UFOs are multi-dimensional and appear and disappear when they "jump" from one dimension to another dimension. Other researchers believe UFO occupants use various frequencies of the electromagnetic spectrum to "cloak" their ships and thus create the illusion of invisibility.

UFOs may use a variety of EM frequencies to "cloak" their visibility and avoid detection. According to Ellen Crystall in her book **Silent Invasion** (Paragon House), "The ships release short wave radiation- ultraviolet, x-ray, and gamma ray - which our eyes do not see but which film registers." Crystall further states, "The ships' external covering has a quality that can render the ship invisible or transparent when lit. The ships' lights illuminate the portion of the ship immediately surrounding the lights. When a ship turns out all its lights, it seems to disappear as if dematerialized, but it has only vanished from our optical view not from our space-time."

UFO contactee George King wrote in his 1964 pamphlet, *The Flying Saucers, A Report on the Flying Saucers, Their Crews and Their Mission to Earth*, "Some vessels from Interplanetary Parliament can be dematerialized at will by their operators and the vibratory octave of their existence so changed as to become invisible to our eyesight. The phenomena has been noted on numerous occasions by aircraft which have been pursuing these flying saucers. Invisibility can also be brought about in another way. At times the operators of Scout Vessels and Mother-Ships choose to rotate the streams of photons around their craft in a 360 degree arc, thereby rendering themselves invisible to the ordinary eye."

In 1978, UFO researcher and publisher Timothy Green Beckley was investigating a series of amazing UFO sightings in the area surrounding Warminster, England. Beckley had gone to a remote hillside just outside of town where a number of UFO sightings had recently taken place. He was accompanied by Arthur Shuttlewood, Bob Strong, and Eva Alcock.

During their hour-long watch on the hill Beckley took a photo of Bob Strong and Eva Alcock. Later, when the picture was developed, Beckley discovered a strange fleeting object behind the people in the photo. "There were no lights out there in the field. It was pitch black, yet there appears to be a bright form moving around in the background that comes down straight out of the sky." Apparently the camera had managed to catch something that was invisible to the human eye.

The use of EM frequencies to mask visibility may also be used by UFO occupants while outside the UFO. In a conscious encounter including multiple witnesses, photographs taken during the event display the image of a being with large, black eyes standing not more than 6-7 feet from the witness who took the photographs. However, according to the same witness, no such being was observed during the encounter. The photographer was actually attempting to photograph another being clearly visible and further away. The being in the photograph was not visible to the naked eye but was registered on film.

Another interesting case involving a strange image caught on film is the so-called "Cumbrian photograph." In 1964, Jim Templeton, a fire officer in the Cumbrain, England Fire Service, took a series of photographs while on a picnic with his family in the Burgh Marsh, a local Cumbrian beauty spot.

When the film was developed, the prints revealed something that was not seen at the time the picture was taken. The photo is of Templeton's five year old daughter, Elizabeth. What makes the picture so strange is that also seen in the background is a figure dressed in what appears to be a white "spacesuit" and wearing a helmet. Jim Templeton said he was "flabbergasted." The only other people around were two ladies who sat in their car some three or four hundred yards away. Templeton recalled that the quiet was unusual. Normally there would be cows and sheep grazing everywhere. However on that particular day the only animals to be seen were huddled on the far side of the marsh.

The film company Kodak became involved with the photograph, even offering free film for life to anyone who could explain the picture, since they could find no evidence that the negative had been tampered with. Whatever it was that Jim Templeton accidentally caught on film that day, it evidently was invisible to the naked eye. Who or what on Earth has that kind of ability?

One theory often neglected in popular UFO literature concerns the reflective surface of UFOs often described by witnesses. Many observers describe UFOs as "mirror-like", "shiny", "reflective" and "like polished metal." The original sighting by Kenneth Arnold in June of 1947 of nine UFOs over Mt. Ranier was typical of reports of highly reflective UFOs: "Every few seconds, two or three of them would dip or change their course slightly, just enough for the sun to catch their reflective surfaces."

Abductees also report observing UFOs with reflective surfaces during abduction experiences. In a childhood abduction, Betty Andreasson-Luca observed a round ship that was, "...silvery, sort of mirror-like and transparent, and trees seemed to reflect in it." During his 1975 abduction experience, Travis Walton reported being taken to a larger ship where he observed various reflective objects in a hangar like room. Walton remembered, "On my left, toward one end of the large room, there were two or three oval-shaped saucers, reflecting light like highly polished chrome. I saw beyond the edge of the brushed-metal craft a silvery reflection that could have been another shiny, rounded craft."

UFOs may also use reflective properties to camouflage their presence and "blend in" with surroundings to avoid observation by human witnesses.

LEVITATION AND INVISIBILITY

Silvery, mirror-like surfaces would naturally reflect blue skies or other surroundings rendering the object virtually invisible. Unfortunately, the closer these objects come to light sources, such as the sun's corona, the less "camouflaged" these objects become and the easier they are to spot. UFO occupants may use all kinds of advanced technology to "cloak" their ships but we must not overlook the simple technique of camouflage used by even the tiniest of Nature's creatures.

UFOs may be rendered invisible through multidimensional travel, electromagnetic frequencies that "cloak" the objects, travel at speeds faster than the human eye can detect and even the use of reflective properties which serve to camouflage these objects. UFOs may not be invisible but rather unvisible to the human eye. As photographs and new techniques demonstrate, UFOs can become visible if we extend the visual range of the human eye through technology and other techniques. We may be looking right at the evidence but not seeing it. All we need now are the right tools to see beyond our physical, and sometimes mental limitations. To induce Invisibility in matter, several techniques have been scientifically proven to accomplish that goal.

1. Bending light around the object so that it cannot contact the object and thus reflect back to the viewer. This principle takes advantage of the Refractive Index of a mass. All matter either reflects diffuses or transmits light (indeed all radiation) to varying degrees based on its Refractive Index.

Refraction refers specifically to the change in direction of radiation, especially light, or sound frequencies as it passes obliquely from one medium to another resulting in a different propagation velocity. This change in the velocity (speed and direction) of the wave causes a corresponding change in the effective wavelength, thus the frequency of the radiation changes while moving within the medium. The degree of change is thus the Refractive Index.

The Refractive Index is the phase velocity of radiation if free space is divided by the phase velocity of the same radiation in a specified medium. The absolute index for all ordinary transparent substances is greater than 1, but there are some special cases (X-rays and light in metal films) for which the index of refraction is less than unity.

Now, if a means of "bending" all incoming visible wavelengths around an object were used, it would become invisible. The movie Predator takes this approach in the cloaking device which the alien wears. It could take the form of a fiber optic mesh or an electronic banding effect. If a high field density magnetic field is used, it would produce life altering effects on both the operator and the environment. Gravity waves might also be used to bend light around a person, thus creating invisibility.

Another method would be the use of a chemical, like that used in the movie "The Invisible Man." Hopefully the effect would be non-toxic and wear off as the body eliminated the chemical over time.

As of now, there are no light-bending techniques which have worked. It is always possible that some researcher or group of researchers has achieved this and is keeping it quiet.

2. Shifting to a higher form of energy which cannot be seen. There is mention of a technique related to possible invisibility fields produced by UFOs. It involves the stimulation of a mass to a frequency in either the Infrared, Ultraviolet or higher frequencies. There are several interesting points when looking at it from this angle, ultraviolet (UV) light sucks heat from the body while infrared (IR) light projects heat into the body. If all visible light reflected from an object could be stepped up to a doubling or a harmonic outside the bounds of the visible spectrum (this could be either Ultra or Infra), then the object would appear as a black hole in the shape of the object.

If IR was used, then the object would give off heat. If UV was used, people in the presence of the operator would experience burns and conjunctivitis (burning, reddening and swelling of the eyes). Many UFO close encounters have as a physical side effect, the burning of the skin and eye swelling. This indicates a high proportion of UV or other higher radiation.

To cause the body to emit frequencies beyond the visible spectrum, one could use a super-heterodyne effect or some form of doubling or tripling. Crystals could be used for achieving the doubling. While super- heterodyning would be accomplished by the blending of two or more frequencies to generate both the sum and difference frequencies.

I don't see how this technique could work if the sole result is to delineate a black human shape. The invisibility would be defeated since the object would be so obvious, if not totally conspicuous.

There is the possibility that there are principles of light which we don't completely understand. This could be especially true at Ultraviolet, Infrared, and other unseen frequencies. For that reason, this possible technique should be looked into.

3. Dimensional shifting of the object itself. If the object could be so "excited" as to translate to a higher dimension or level of being, then it would effectively not be respondent to radiations, including light, from this dimension. One case involved certain experiments using high density fluctuating magnetic fields.

A device was built in the shape of a split-phase coil with many turns of wire. When the subject sat astraddle the coil and the power was applied, at certain frequencies and magnetic field densities, the subject saw the room slowly vanish to be displaced by other scenery.

Further experiments caused the subject and the coil to begin to vanish from the test area. The subject obviously "translated" to a higher dimension, both visually and physically. This might not be the rule for all such experiments. There is much work to be done using different frequencies, combinations of such and field densities. It might be possible to cause a "vanishing" without losing the physical form. One of the communications given to UFO contact Billy Meier stated that the Pleidians used a time shifting technique. This allowed them to vanish and reappear in another location almost instantly.

They said time could be divided into many separate and distinct moments, each of which could house an entire universe co-existent with ours, yet totally unknown and unsuspected by us. Perhaps this theory explains how UFO's, Bigfoot, Loch Ness and other anomalies occur in our reality. They are momentarily "displaced" entities from another dimension.

It would follow that phase conjugate techniques could be used to energize an area to a level of very high field density. If something walked into that field as it "scanned" another dimension, it could be "charged" to forcibly drag it into our dimension. When this occurs, the being is disturbed and confused by this seemingly "magical" accident.

As time progressed, the energy charge would fade away and the entity would reach the quantum level necessary to cause the return to their home dimension. This of course could work the other way. Perhaps some of the thousands of people who turn up missing each year have been carried into some other dimension, never to be seen again.

Writer, Arthur Shuttlewood experienced numerous UFO-related phenomenons while investigating the UFO flap over Warminster, England in 1972. Some of his unusual sightings involved UFOs and weird creatures that seemed to utilize invisibility of some kind. "Events of the last few months have helped to steadily convince me that a sizeable portion of what has transpired in and around Warminster, is of a non-physical nature, totally defying the laws of science. We now have strong evidence that some of these aeroforms are capable of making themselves invisible."

Shuttlewood maintained that under certain circumstances these "invisible" UFOs and their crew members can be seen with the aid of photographic equipment or by individuals who happen to visually catch them while they are in the process of making a transformation from visibility to invisibility.

During the winter of 1972, Shuttlewood was able to see for himself the strange nature of the mysterious visitors.

"It was about 8:30PM. I was on Starr Hill along with a half-dozen other individuals, including a former police officer and a bank executive. Suddenly, we heard thumping noises from a clump of bushes to our left. Another sound caused us all to look at the hedgerow to our left. That's when we saw the three giant figures standing at the edge of a field some distance away. They were all eight feet tall, had domed heads, no apparent necks, wide shoulders, and long arms that dangled at their sides. Their outlines were clearly discernible even though it was dark; the strange thing was that you could see right through them."

As the startled observers attempted to leave the area the transparent "creatures" followed them, gliding several inches above the ground.

"We attempted to communicate with them, but they did not respond. A member of our party walked right up to one of these beings and was able to pass right through the eerie form. The figures vanished as the lights of approaching cars moved in our direction."

Sightings of transparent creatures around the nearby Cradle Hill were also reported. Sally Pike, daughter of retired Police Superintendent John Rossiter, gave the following details of her strange experiences.

"Both my husband and I have had rather unnerving experiences at Cradle Hill. One evening, I saw quite clearly the outline of a tall male figure striding up the road in the bright moonlight. He seemed about seven feet tall, with extremely long arms. His body itself, only the outline being solid, was almost transparent and silverish. As I watched, he slowly faded away and completely vanished."

Mrs. Pike's husband, Neal, would encounter a similar being several days later.

"As I approached the white metal gates which lead to Cradle Hill, I suddenly saw three giant figures standing in a line. At first they were mere shadowy, ghostlike outlines. But, as I peered through the darkness, they sharpened their form until they appeared almost solid. The unusual thing was that their bodies disappeared at the mid-section. Their legs and feet were invisible."

Wondering if his eyes were playing tricks on him, Neal aimed his flashlight at one of the creatures. Immediately the giant vanished, only to reappear at another spot.

LEVITATION AND INVISIBILITY

"I flashed my searchlight onto the two other forms, and the same thing happened. The ghostly trio was now much closer to me, their faces featureless, black and fearsome."

Neal Pike decided that he had seen enough, and quickly fled Cradle Hill.

Research done by Shuttlewood showed that a total of seventeen people had seen the gigantic, transparent beings on Cradle and Starr Hills.

"There was something strange going on in Warminster. It may be that an armada of spaceships and their crews were using our town as a landing base or way station. There is now substantial evidence to indicate that they are able to make themselves invisible upon command. We can only guess as to what their purpose might be. Let us hope it is a peaceful one."

In his book *UFO Chronicles of the Soviet Union*, veteran ufologist Jacques Vallee describes a UFO landing in a park in the Soviet city of Voronezh in full view of children playing soccer there, as well as about forty adults. After the craft had landed, a very tall three-eyed being and a robotic entity emerged and started moving around. When a nearby boy cried out in fear, and other people started shouting, the beings and the UFO vanished on the spot.

As Vallee writes: "Five minutes later the sphere and the three-eyed being appeared again, just as strangely as they had disappeared. The being now had at his side a tube about four feet in length. A sixteen-year-old boy was close to the scene. The alien pointed his 'rifle' toward the teenager, and the boy instantly disappeared. The alien entered the sphere and the sphere flew away, gradually increasing its speed. At the same instant the vanished teenager reappeared."

It would be interesting to know whether the boy was physically there, yet invisible, during this experience or whether he was somehow not there, in which case, where was he, how did he get back, and what did the experience feel like to him? Additional questions would relate to the physics of the UFO's invisibility, and the alien's tube. Nevertheless, we can be sure that, while public science cannot at present explain this phenomenon, the military would be extremely interested in it, and there are probably numerous parents the world over who at times would love to own one of the alien's invisible-making tubes.

UFOnauts have obviously mastered the art of invisibility as well as levitation. Eyewitnesses have seen visitors from outer space levitating outside their spaceships. Earthlings have experienced being levitated from the ground and into the opening of ships for visits. UFOs on the ground have been seen to rise up without the use of any power, rocket or otherwise. How is it done? Is levitation too far-fetched an answer? We think not.

LEVITATION AND INVISIBILITY

FLYING SAUCERS FROM A SCIENTIFIC POINT OF VIEW
By Nikolai Noskov

Translated from the original Russian by Yury SARYCHEV
English text edited by Christopher Bjerknes

Pamphlets concerning UFO's and dozens of clippings from every conceivable newspaper replete with communications from, and evidence of UFO's, contact with the "humanoids", wrecked "flying saucers"; and regarding research into the remains of aliens in the USA; lie before me on my desk. UFO's have been discussed in the United Nations. Serious scientists in several countries have devoted a large portion of their lives to analyzing the various aspects of this question.

Within Russia and the nations of the UIS, the questions presented by UFO's have been studied for some 50 years. Research scientist Yury Fomin has written, "The number of sightings of UFO's increases each year. There have already been hundreds of thousands of reports of UFO's. Diverse messages are received on every continent. At the conclusion of the fiftieth year, it is apparent that there is a contradiction between the facts regarding UFO sightings and their incompatibility with our present understanding of physical phenomena... We have probably plunged head-first into new qualitative categories, which cannot be reconciled with our current beliefs, with our present world view... It is impossible for a person to understand the operating principle of an electric motor, unless he or she has a basic knowledge of electromagnetism".

This last phrase aptly demonstrates why the many attempts at exposing the underlying principles of the phenomenon of UFO's have all failed. The phrase symbolizes the extent to which modern researchers have abandoned practical materialistic philosophy, and have instead deluded themselves with the mathematical formalism of relativistic physics to so great a degree that they are unable to reach logical conclusions, for they have isolated themselves from the reality of the physical processes involved. These researchers have surrounded themselves with a formalistic fog, which blinds them to the subject of their research.

First of all, since the goal of science is to find the "one among the many," as Plato wrote, or the identities between diverse phenomena which comprise the categories of qualitative analysis, it is poor method to devise new and purely abstract ad hoc qualitative categories simply to explain the properties and behavior of UFO's, especially since said properties and behaviors are easily described through the most general principles of empirical method, as opposed to formalistic fantasy. The facts are readily explainable by means of our present knowledge. However, our view of reality is obstructed by the many ad hoc hypotheses, the jargon and the false concepts of relativistic physics. Secondly, though Fomin boasted that he and other modern physicists fully understand the operating principle of an electric motor, in that they have a fundamental knowledge of electromagnetism, nothing could be further from the truth. Our knowledge of electromagnetism is restricted to a certain set of empirical formulas and rules, such as the right-hand and left-hand rules for conductors and charges moving through a cross-section of magnetic flux, etc. Certainly, that is not the operating principle of an electric motor.

And thirdly, it is easy to explain any phenomenon, especially from the perspective of relativistic physics, since, according to Feynman, with "anything" it is possible to explain "everything". He, unfortunately, widely employed this method, having left us a world-wide legacy of a "noting" school of elementary particle physics, by which method it is safe to assume that the humanoids have learned to "penetrate space-time" and arrive here from the 12th-dimension by means of anti-gravitation or some such thing. On our planet, we have a number of physicists, who develop theories of 12-dimensional spaces, superstrings and other such "miracles". However, should they attempt to prove the existence of dimensions beyond the third, they will not, and cannot, succeed, since science and pure fantasy are incompatible.

Science is the method of establishing the connections between the phenomena of the material world and its causes and corollaries. It is the discovery of the laws of Nature through logical inference and deduction based on the fullest set of observations, facts and experiments currently available to the scientist. It is not knowledge known a priori. There must be substantial proof of the failure of an established category and the necessity of a new category, before it is reasonable to posit a new categorical invariant, in the same class as space, time or mass. The misbegotten introduction of a new invariant velocity of light, c, has led physicists to act on faith and resulted in a vulgar mathematical formalism.

In previously published articles ("Science of Kazakhstan", #56, 65, 73) I argued against the internal inconsistencies of relativistic physics, which violate formal method in both electrodynamics and quantum mechanics. Returning to classical mechanics with its invariants and causality, allows me to form a hypothesis regarding the mechanism of a UFO. This hypothesis fully describes the "fantastic" properties of the phenomenon, but does not resort to pseudo-scientific fantasies; and the hypothesis can be tested by means of experiment.

James Clerk Maxwell set forth a set of equations for the jet engine of a "flying saucer" ca. 1861...1862. In fact, he modeled motions and tensions in the ether in order to describe electromagnetic phenomena. It is certain that he did not have "flying saucers" in mind. These equations attained their modern form in the hands of J. J. Thomson, H. Hertz, O. Heaviside and H. A. Lorentz. No one, however, realized the efficacy of an "ethereal scaffold", until now. The electrodynamic equations of Maxwell and Hertz implicitly contain the equations of a jet engine, with the ether's serving as a propulsive agent. This engine can be roughly understood in the following way, having simulated a vortex in the form of a magnetic field, existing in proximity to a conductor carrying current, it is possible to eventually obtain an efflux of ether along its axis. The development of an efflux of ether will take place in various phases and result in rather interesting phenomena, as follows:

> Luminescence, polarized rays, electrical and magnetic fields; Optical effects, such as the blurring of the outlines and the complete invisibility of the spacecraft; Effects of attraction (traction), or repulsion (pressure); Non-inertial motion (reduction of force of inertia).

If the ether is defined as the medium for light waves and the seat of electrical and magnetic phenomena, we can readily explain the first three points. As to the fourth point, here we must address the phenomenon of inertial motion, i.e. Galilean relativity.

Inertia is an interaction between bodies and the ether. Should the ether ahead of a moving body become rarefied (as in this case, where the ethereal jet engine takes in the ether in its direction of motion), the force of inertia will be considerably reduced, permitting the body to accelerate rapidly, without becoming overloaded, and without consuming a great deal of energy.

The engineering of such a vehicle will be different from what we are accustomed to seeing in "modern" vehicles. The only moving part is a thin metal sheet rolled into the form of a cylinder and composed of rare earth elements (forming a strong permanent ring-shaped magnet). It can rotate without coming into contract with any other parts (on magnetically lubricated bearings). Theoretically, it is possible to instigate the rotation of a magnetic cylinder by passing a current through its axis...

Having no notion of the method of operation of an ethereal engine, our earthly mechanic, upon examining one, will be nonplussed. There is no burner, nor nozzles, nor transmission gears... Incidentally, a disk-shape is the most efficient form for an ethereal jet engine. The rotation of a magnetic cylinder creates a vacuum of ether fore, and a pressure aft, which pressure differential impels the vehicle forward.

Light waves and other electromagnetic radiation emitted from the machine disappear in the rarefied ether. Rarefied ether is a poor conductor of electromagnetic oscillations, just as rarefied air is a poor conductor for sound.

LEVITATION AND INVISIBILITY

Therefore, the vehicle cannot be seen as it approaches. The nervous systems of human beings and of animals are conductors of electrical signals, which connect all the living cells of an organism. The human brain is a very complex computer, in which electromagnetic phenomena also take place. It is not surprising that aliens must, of necessity, dress in protective garb, which clothing shields them from the powerful and destructive electrical and magnetic fields. The aliens, who are aware of the disastrous effects of electrical fields on living organisms, avoid close landings and flyovers in close proximity to highly populated regions. In order to minimize the risks to living organisms, they land only at night.

A "flying saucer" can potentially be of any size, from a small arm firing a projectile by means of an electrical field, through a backpack propulsion device for personal mobility in the atmosphere, up to a full-sized spacecraft. The hi-tech nature of the technology of the magnetic cylinder and control circuitry belies the utter simplicity of the mechanism. The magnetic cylinder should be constructed of high-strength magnetic material of uniform thickness, which achieves the Curie point at a high temperature.

By virtue of the recorded data from astronomical observation and the results of astrogeological surveys, we have reason to believe that the Galaxy evolves outward from the center (germ) of mass, expanding step-by-step out to the periphery, initially throwing out space dust, which dust then forms into stars. These new stars repel the space dust, which then forms into new stars... and this process repeats itself in each new layer forming in the cycle during which the stars are approximately the size of our Sun.

Each star, spewing "superfluous" mass into space, concurrently forms its own planetary system. The creation, evolution and existence of planetary systems occurs with strict physical regularity, and those systems which are nearer the periphery of a Galaxy, are the more recently developed systems.

Stars, of necessity, form planetary systems. Since we are on the periphery of a Galaxy, it follows that our Solar System is one of the youngest. The elementary composition, as well as the size of planets in a planetary system, obey Maxwell's distribution of energies of ejected matter by a central star and the fundamental laws of quantum gravitation. As a result, if the elementary structure of two stars is similar, then their planetary systems should likewise be similar. Given this identity, it is likely that the second, third or fourth planet of each star is populated with a living and aware creature like man. Mankind evolves under certain general laws. If we assume that the neighboring layer of stars arranged toward the center of a Galaxy evolved millions of years before those further from center, then it is safe to assume that some civilizations are older than ours.

71

LEVITATION AND INVISIBILITY

Given the frequency and variety of UFO visitations on the Earth, we may conclude that they reach us from several layers of stars in the vicinity of our solar system. To them, our civilization must seem not only socially primitive, but technologically primitive, as well. Their expeditions are probably made for utilitarian reasons: to explore the vast array of living forms, to view the past, to catalog another civilization, to make an intermediate landing, etc. I would guess that we are fascinated by them, because our science and technology have been surpassed by a trivial physical phenomenon, which forms the basis for the mechanism of a flying saucer, while we excel only in internal combustion engines, rockets burning solid and liquid fuel, atomic energy...

This article was previously published in: "*Science of Kazakhstan*", 1 (99), August 1...15, 1997.

DECLASSIFIED MILITARY DOCUMENTS INDICATE HIGH LEVEL OF INTEREST IN UFO INVISIBILITY

The fact that there have been many cases of UFOs being seen either seemingly appearing out of nowhere, or completely vanishing in the blink of an eye, has not gone unnoticed by the military of several countries.

When the UK began releasing their once classified UFO documents, researchers discovered this interesting bit of information that had been sent to Geoffrey Hoan, Secretary of State for Air on September 8 2000.

To:

Geoffrey Hoan. Secretary of State for Air.

Whitehall. London:

Strictly Confidential

Sir,

Please see the above 'websites' – you may find the contents very difficult to believe, or accept, I CAN only say that they are the truth, the whole truth and nothing but the truth ... whether you believe that statement, or not, is out of my hands.

The difficulties in 'accepting' such 'out of this world' material I thoroughly understand ... I had the same difficulties in the early days of this 'communication', but that was nearly twenty years ago .... (incidentally, II reported my first 'saucer sighting', in 1954, to the Air Ministry in Whitehall. in the Summer of '54 (a long time ago). However, in my work, which has gone on constantly for almost twenty years, I have been given a great deal of information that could not be acquired in any other way than I use.... a few days ago I received the enclosed 'technical information on "How can UFOs become invisible?" .... this appears to be quite remarkable information ... and confirms my opinion that 'they' are vastly in advance of anything WE regard as 'human'.

In your position you must know of the thousands of UFO 'sightings' throughout the world ... daily, and constantly ... (! get an 'international report' of incidents, world-wide, every three weeks or so, of every unusual event in the UFO story there are dozens every week.

Please read the section enclosed on 'invisibility and. if you can, pass it to some of your scientific experts on aircraft possibilities ... I would like to hear their comments, of course. If you have any questions please contact me, on Email if you wish.

Contained with this letter was this interesting document.

How Can UFOs Become Invisible?

Spacecraft can become 'invisible' due to a projected electromagnetic shield. rotating at the speed of light, it is made up of six atomic reflectors working in complementary pairs. This shield is projected from the center of the shielded area, within the craft.

Reflectors have the thickness of one atom, each having a static charge, alternately negative and positive to maintaining equal distances between them. At 90 degrees to the plane any wave form will pass through, but at an angle it will be reflected. A fixed relationship is maintained in positioning to prevent warping of time or distance.

Of the 6 reflectors, 2 are particle, or frequency, accelerators, 2 are excited as to decelerate reflected frequencies and the remaining 2 are passive, or standard, reflectors. Acceleration and deceleration are achieved by electro-magnetic energy transfer, like a high frequency alternating current. Passive and decelerating reflectors are equal in length, but longer than the accelerating reflectors, the length ratio being slightly more than 1.2071 to 1 The acceleration rate is slightly less than 85 percent (at the second reflector pair) with a converse deceleration rate at the final reflector pair.

LEVITATION AND INVISIBILITY

Accelerating reflectors are in link with the Horizontal plane and decelerating reflectors, as like passive reflectors, are set at exactly 22.5   degrees to the horizontal.

There are 3 complementary reflective sequences. the first reflection is passive, the second accelerates and the third decelerates.

In development of this technology you would find, in practical application, that if the more logical sequence of 'accelerate. reflect, decelerate' were followed then efficiency would be halved due to the increased distance covered by the accelerated particles.

Relationships between reflective lengths and positions of each   reflector is dependent on the size of area to be hidden. If reflector were too long, or too close, a 'dark' area would be detected.

If they were too short, or too far apart, the shielded area would be detected as only partly obscuring, length and position have a theoretical tolerance . If one atom.

N.B. The reflective shield, or electro-magnetic field. adds to stability of the craft and assists in maneuvering at high speed with sudden changes in direction.

Terms used here are simple and comprehensive. The 'expert' may note the relationship with Einstein's theory of relativity, after close analysis of the figures given, which, incidentally, obeys the same laws as the surface area of a circle.

The possibility that some UFOs are capable of achieving optical invisibility is evident from reported cases such as radar/non-visual reports in which radar clearly indicated a moving, physical object, while observation of the sky showed nothing. The question is, how does an invisible object manage to reflect radar signals, yet be able to allow light to either "go around" or even through them. Is it reasonable to suggest that a UFO and its crew is able to become completely transparent to the visible light spectrum?

QIGONG AND UFOs

Qigong is pronounced 'Chi Koong' and some people also spell it Chi Kung or Qi Gong (or even Qui Gong, which is wrong). It is an ancient form of Chinese remedial exercise which is preventative, healing, relaxing, meditative,

74

gentle and accessible to all ages and sexes. Qigong is part of traditional Chinese medicine and is an excellent self-healing treatment. It doesn't cost anything to perform, requires no equipment, takes up little space, and most of its many styles may be learned in no time.

There are many definitions of Qigong but they all agree that: any practice involving the mind, body and breathing which can reinforce and balance life energy could be defined as Qigong. Such as, for instance, relaxation, yoga, meditation, Reiki, chanting or breathing techniques. To the Chinese these are all forms of Qigong. This can be said because the regular practice of any of the above has similar results. Yet, some styles of Qigong, rarely or never heard of in the west, are known to bring extraordinary results.

The word "Qi" (chi) means life force (energy). "Gong" means ability, or skill. Combined the words translate to mean practicing life force (energy), or, rebalancing it. And because "Qi" also means breath, or breathing, it's often translated as Qigong Breathing.

Now, you may say, why should I do Qigong? Or what is this new practice - Qigong? Amazingly enough it is not new at all, in fact it is thousands of years old. And you do it without even knowing it. Animals do it too!!!!!! Many Qigong styles are taken or learned directly from animals (you can find more on that subject in other sections of our website).

So, every time we relax our mind and body, rest, sleep, take a stroll through nature, when we are without a care in the world, or responding to emotion as nature intended, that is crying from grief, shouting in anger or laughing from joy, we are doing Qigong. When we injure ourselves and yell 'ouch', or pray, or sing for joy, dance in high spirits, we are doing some sort of rebalancing, in other words practicing Qigong.

But when we deliberately practice some advanced forms of Qigong we can know for sure that we are rebalancing our energies in a systematic way. And if we practice regularly and persistently, day after day, we will get results, great results and more. The regular practice of Qigong, not only maintains health, but its good effects flow on into whatever we do, increasing productivity and levels of accomplishment.

There are countless styles of Qigong and it would take many life times to learn them all. Fortunately, we need learn only one to achieve everything we need.

Most human beings are basically influenced by their senses, such as hearing, sight, taste, touch and smell and it is to these factors we continually react and are strongly influenced by. Unless we undertake to elevate our levels of consciousness with Qigong.

LEVITATION AND INVISIBILITY

In the west we put a lot of emphasis on the brain, the logical mind and its ability to analyze and reach a conclusion. But intellectual reasoning is far from wisdom and higher consciousness.

Qigong has the ability to help us transcend the senses and reach a higher state of consciousness or, in other words, develop higher levels of energy where mind (or the energy of thought) can control matter (i.e. change their structure, move them around etc.). There are Qigong masters, people who have practiced Qigong all their lives, who are renowned for their wisdom and freedom from material desires. Their lives, the way they live and act, are a silent witness to the freeing power of Qigong.

Qigong breathing has a long history. Some say it is a million years old, in fact there are records of it which go back to when writing was invented. Yet, it has never been so popular as it is now in China. Literally millions of Chinese practice some form of Qigong every day of their life and the official word is, Qigong has saved the government billions of dollars.

There are many different styles or forms of Qigong. There are at least five major sources of it. The Buddhists have about 70,000 styles, the Taoists about 30,000, then there are thousands of Kung Fu and Chinese medicine styles and hundreds of Confucian styles. So you can see it is not short on forms.

The beauty of Qigong is that there are styles to suit all ages, and all states of health, even people who are too weak to get out of bed or sit up. As long as a person can follow directions mentally they can do Qigong and get results. What is important to understand is that Qigong can bring great and unexpected results, but not always quickly. Qigong usually works slowly and steadily despite the fact that many people can have major results amazingly quickly.

It has been proven over many years, with many millions of cases, particularly in China, that if Qigong is practiced, it can provide definite healing effects. However, Qigong is much more than just a healing aid.

The healing aspect of Qigong goes to the lowest fundamental level, that it is possible to reach, because according to traditional Chinese medicine, disease is a result of an imbalance in the body's Qi (life energy). The practice of Qigong over a period of time restores the energy balance. Once the balance of Qi energy is established in the body, there is an automatic healing process, where the metabolism of the patient is restored, often with varying periods of time, depending on the complex nature of the imbalance and which meridians have been blocked.

It is only after the energy is in a balanced state and the person is in good health again that he or she is able to move to higher levels of Qigong. To reach the higher levels, may take some years to achieve, and is dependent on the amount of practice and the sincere intent of the person to reach it. The style of Qigong that a person does, also affects the extent to which the person achieves a higher level.

Many great masters of Qigong have a lot in common, regardless of what style they practice. They are all, to a greater or lesser extent, able to carry out the following: mind healing comprising direct healing, involving concentration or focusing the mind onto a problem, mass healing, remote diagnosing, remote healing, teleporting or using the mind to transport objects from one place to another, telepathy, predicting the future and many other unusual abilities.

Some other unique abilities that only some Qigong masters possess would be: The ability to talk to animals or to make animals come to a certain place at a certain time even if such animals would not normally come to that requested place, e.g. snakes, wolves, foxes, eagles and many others to come to someone's garden.

Some Qigong masters are able to effect changes to weather conditions. They are able to generate clouds and make rain, or if it is cloudy they can return the weather to being bright and sunny.

Some by mind focusing can join or cut heavy items such as bars or sheets of metal, wood or heavy paper. Such dedication to the practice of Qigong also enables some masters to be able to pass through solid walls or to become invisible. Etc., etc.

All of the above, no matter how unbelievable it may seem, have been witnessed by many people and have been the subject of scientific research in China for over twenty years, involving reputable scientists and institutions.

One of the well-known Qigong masters from Guangdong Province in China, Master Lin Qingquan developed a strange ability which enabled him to write stories and novels whilst in a Qigong state. He has already published more than twenty fictional works that are mainly concerned with the UFO's, aliens and the deep mysteries of the universe. His books are presented in an amazing orderliness where the matters he describes appear in a very logical manner.

Unlike the usual Western style science fiction novels, which are often written by people who have a very artificial view on the matter and who often use their imagination to prepare their stories so that their readers are left with a low level of creditability, with many obvious errors in structure and substance involving English speaking aliens that have human habits, Master Lin displays an in depth logic and an impression that he has personally experienced the matter he is writing about.

LEVITATION AND INVISIBILITY

What is even more strange about the way in which Master Lin prepares his novels is that they are written in finished format within a very short period of time, say overnight. In other words there is no rough draft or proofreading required. It is as though Master Lin, when entering the Qigong state, connects with some other existing world which he absorbs and then converts into a simple written and understandable form.

The only conscious thing about his work is his desire to write about a certain subject, and the rest is all a result of the practice. In other words, before he enters his Qigong state, he might request the information to a certain question, such as "what type of life is there on planet X?" for instance, and then his pen becomes the writer, he is merely the one holding it. It is almost like surfing the internet, where you can do a search on a particular subject by entering the subject name or related words.

In most cases the only way that one can ever achieve similar experiences with Qigong is by consistent practice over a long period of time. One first learns to stop the brain and all the senses (ie using consciousness) so that they reach total blankness and detachment and then at that level of knowing nothing, they start to know everything (ie using their sub-consciousness).

Master Lin however, didn't stop there. Apart from writing books, he established a research institute and school to examine the mysteries of supernatural events and to research alien civilizations and alien technology. His work has already attracted the attention of many individuals and institutions and he has earned himself an interesting title " Strange Man of Present Age."

Master Lin works hard on his ideas working sixteen hours a day, seven days a week, but always remains fresh in mind and full of energy, which is a typical characteristic of high-level Qigong masters. They tend to require little sleep and can perform a lot more than other people, they never tire.

Master Lin explains that his ability to achieve the high level of Qigong that he has attained is explained by the fact that he began to practice Qigong early in life. Firstly, he achieved an ability to heal others for which he has become renowned, and remains so. Then he discovered the power of his sub-consciousness, allowing him to surf the Qigong Internet. All this lead to an increasing interest in extra-terrestrials and other mysteries of the universe. Among his books are titles such as: *Flying Saucers & Aliens, Negative Physics, Qigong Awakening, Notes of the Soul, Zen in the Depth of the Night, Who am I, Oriental Art & Imagery*. Many critics agree that, in the areas he concentrates, his quality of work is excellent.

Are there aliens in the world? Or rather in the universe? (The latter is much easier to answer. We know for sure there are because we are all aliens).

LEVITATION AND INVISIBILITY

Well, we don't know for sure, but if they do exist, they definitely practice Qigong. "What the...," will probably be your first reaction. After you calm down and (if you) keep reading, you might think again. There are already so many books, magazines, videos and TV programs on the subject and if you are interested enough we're sure you'll find something. All we're saying is that, if only one percent of that is true, we have strong reason to believe there are aliens among us. Especially when you take into account almost identical stories of people with different backgrounds who could not possibly know each other, who claim they were abducted by aliens. In many cases research was done not only by reputable scientists, but also on people highly regarded in their community.

Plus all the unexplained things in the world that tell us that whoever did them, were not humans. Such as the pyramids of Egypt built thousands of years ago, out of huge stone blocks, in the middle of the desert, where there is nothing but sand, while we are still not able to construct them today in such proportions. Or the huge crop circles that keep occurring overnight every year in different parts of the world, so precisely and so neatly constructed. Not to mention Roswell where, despite numerous witnesses and pressure from all sides (based on our "right to know") until today, the US government never shared their complete report on the incident that happened in the 40's. It's not the first time that truth (for some reason) is being hidden in front of our very eyes. And so, as our children continue to learn at school that pyramids were built by Egyptian slaves, let's see what Qigong masters have to say on the subject.

Unlike most of us, who can only see what is in front of our eyes and what's offered for us on say TV and the internet, masters of Qigong can "see" many things hidden from everybody's eyes. They can even see and hear things that no longer exist or are yet to happen. Remember the Qigong master from Guangzhou who knew so much about aliens that he wrote books and books on the subject. Some Qigong masters proved that they have some kind of connection and communication link with aliens and they describe aliens as energy (chi) superior to all humans including high level masters of Qigong. Or others who know a lot, but for whatever reason, hesitate to share their findings with ordinary people or only on rare occasions hint a thing or two when asked about someone's encounters.

A Qigong master was asked about the origin of aliens. He suggested that there are not only one type of alien on earth, but a few - one that always resided here and others that came from some other planets). Now, regardless of where they came from and what they look like, if you know a little more about Qigong masters and their extraordinary powers, there is one thing that comes to mind right away, once you hear the stories of people who encountered aliens. You'd be very surprised to find that, "apparently", aliens can do all those things that they can, such as use their minds to communicate with each other, read other people's minds, control objects, animals and people (e.g. make objects move, jump, levitate, paralyze people), teleport objects, people or themselves (i.e. disappear from one place and reappear in another), walk through walls, predict the future and see the past (even play it on an invisible screen right in front of your very eyes), play with electric energy, make electric devices work without power etc.

Of course, Qigong masters can treat all sorts of illnesses, which make one wonder that aliens must be great healers as well. Drawing more parallels, it would also mean that they would be detached from material possession, live a very long life, be calm and of very good character. The fact that they, again "apparently", bring people back after abducting them (instead of "having them for dinner") and that with their, more superior technology than ours, they could easily turn us into their slaves, but they don't, demonstrates that. They are obviously interested in getting to know us better before (if ever) they introduce themselves to us "officially" and they are already trying to tell us something before that. Something they know about and we don't. It's probably something that we are doing, that can endanger us more than them.

It's not quite clear whether aliens are born with those abilities, or they acquire them after years of practicing some form of Qigong, like Qigong masters do, however one thing is for sure - they definitely are grand masters of Qigong.

EDI - - - AN OTHER-WORLDLY ENIGMA

Edi lives in South America. She is about 30 years old with a pretty face and rich black hair that tumbles to her waist. Edi is an accountant for a major industry in Bolivia. Ever since she has been old enough to think for herself she has felt that she was put on Earth to carry out a special mission. What that assignment is, is not entirely clear to her as yet. She does have two clues. One is that she is adept at math. The other is a peculiar birthmark on her back. An astronomer has studied the mark and believes that it matches a major constellation in space.

Noted investigator Bill Cox who wrote about Edi in his book, **Unseen Kingdoms** (Inner Light Publications) thinks Edi may actually be a "walk-in," an entity from another world, and that her birthmark is a sign to others that they have found a comrade. Apparently, she is "marked" for a definite reason. Edi has already been contacted by other "walk-ins" who have greeted her without really telling her what her mission is. Edi has some theories of her own, but she refuses to speculate publicly.

For example, a few years ago Edi was stopped on the street by a man in his fifties. He had white hair and a white beard. He had approached her from behind and therefore "saw" the mark on her back. Incredibly, he called her by name, saying, "Edi, you are one of us... you have the birthmark on your back."

Edi had never seen the man before, but the amazing part of the story was that he could not have seen the birthmark because Edi was wearing a dress with covered it.

The man told her, "I'm to give you this book. Keep it as long as you want. It contains the information you need because your work begins as of now."

He told Edi that he was from the same constellation as her, and then showed a birthmark on his arm that matched hers perfectly. Edi read the book, then reread it. The information in it was interesting but not world-shaking. In fact, she kept it in her home for a year and a half before picking it up again.

The message for her was on the first page. She now knew what she had to do. Weeks later she brought the book to work, and on her way home she heard a voice say, "Thank you for returning the book." She turned around and saw a white-bearded man. What perplexed Edi was how the man knew she had the book in her purse. She gave him the book. He then told her, "You will be contacted again soon."

Several months later Edi was in La Paz, Bolivia on an assignment for her employer. She was in a hotel restaurant eating dinner alone and not thinking about much of anything. Suddenly, a man approached her. He was extremely tall, about six feet seven inches, and good looking. He too, knew her name. He said, "Edi, I am glad to see you here, may I sit down?" He smiled at her and continued, "I know about your birthmark. I have one too."

Edi was not thrilled, she intended to say no to the stranger, but he did appear sincere. The blond man said, "I don't want you to think that I wish to invade your mind, but I read your thoughts, and it's OK. Am I correct?" Then he sat down and rolled up his sleeve. The birthmark was on the inside of his left forearm, and it was exactly the same as the one on Edi's back.

The next day the blond man took Edi to an ancient site in Bolivia called Tihuanacu. Archaeologists are puzzled by the ruins. However, UFOlogists believe it is an ancient Initiatic and Sacred Ceremonial city. The feeling is that Tihuanacu was a favorite landing area for ancient astronauts.

By now however, Edi was curious about her new friend. If he were really sent to Earth by a superior power, then he would have to prove it. At her request, the man smiled and promptly levitated his body into the air. Next he levitated a large, heavy stone.

The man said, "Edi, you must now learn the power of your mind. I want you to mentally raise the stone."

The women said, "But I can't levitate things."

"Yes, you can." He raised the stone again, and after a few minutes Edi was able to the same, although it did wobble and sink back to the ground. What she did was to keep the stone levitated after the blond man raised it up, but she was successful in only holding it in the air with his help. He told her that she would learn to do it by herself eventually. Then he took her on a tour of the ruins, explaining how their forefathers landed in that area eon's ago, and used levitation to lift the heavy rocks to build the impressive structures.

Also in **Unseen Kingdoms**, Bill Cox tells about Paul, a South American "spaceman" who is setting up a research center in Brasilia, Brazil.

THE UNCANNY PAUL LAUSSAC - - - SPACEMAN

According to Bill, Paul Laussac is financially secure. What he wants to do is serve humanity. Money is not his goal. Paul has a giving nature. Like most New Age people, he does not chase the dollar, but instead, chases after anything that will improve mankind. For that reason he created the research center.

Paul has the uncanny ability to appear, or not to appear, in any photo taken of him. If he chooses, he will be seen only as energy on film. Bill Cox, who spent a lot of time in South America, says that a few of the spacemen he met in Brazil have the same ability.

Cox says: "I've been in photos with Paul where my own body began to disappear because specialized energy extended from his body into my own auric field. It is hard to get a good picture of him in focus because he is so often in a different state of vibration than we might expect in ordinary human terms.

"Although our naked eye doesn't see these energies," says Cox, "just as the tape recorder in voice tape phenomena records voices and sounds from other dimensions we don't ordinarily hear. In other words, these energies function in the sub-audible or super-audible ranges, giving us extended hearing, and wider vision in the ultra-violet and infra-red spectra. We see only within a very small range of a vastly greater visual scale. There are other octaves of vision. Clairvoyants, clairaudients and certain instruments record frequencies of seeing and hearing that have little to do with infra-red or ultra-violet. They are obviously registering sights and sounds perceived in the higher octaves of light and color, music and sound. People with ultra-sensitive hearing may be clairaudient, that is, hearing broadcasts without radio; voices and music from the spheres."

These energy forms that appear are made up of elemental forces or spirits. For example, there are three types of fire. Electrical fire is the highest, then solar fire, and fire by friction. Spontaneous combustion or chemical fire comes under the classification of solar fire. All three fires operate as a result of fire electricity, produce heat and in the highest aspect, is electricity. Paul is likely operating in the solar realm, though we don't have any instruments sensitive enough to measure it.

I call people like Paul, spacemen for lack of a more specific or appropriate term. They come from our planetary existence in many ways. Not all enter our world in UFOs or spacecraft of a physical kind, some are born here, or later on, have taken over a body, often a damaged one, quickly repairing it with unimaginable healing skills. The personality emerges in a person who now demonstrates marvelous powers. These are all incarnating souls coming from somewhere in space, hence the term spaceman/woman.

ACHIEVING INVISIBILITY INSIDE A PYRAMID

Bill Cox published a newsletter called *The Pyramid Guide*. He's had letters from all over the world, and has had people visit him to learn more about the magic of the pyramid.

About six years ago some California architects asked him to meet with them at Pepperdine University in Malibu. They had built an interlaced, rod framework of tetrahedrons which made up a pyramid about 30 feet high. It was covered with nylon. Bill Cox told me that he frequently gets a photographic phenomenon under a pyramid in which it appears that the individuals being photographed are becoming invisible.

He calls this "solarization." He says that the subjects inside and outside the pyramid are in different states of vibration. The body energy of those inside alters the photographic result. For some reason, a solarization effect takes place on the film, but the boundaries of that effect are restricted to bodies only. If this had been due to defects on the film, or processing errors, the entire photo frame would exhibit solarization throughout. This is not the case. One photo clearly shows three individuals actually fading from view, although the rest of the picture is perfectly clear. Ancient Egyptian legends state that those who knew the secret, could become invisible by entering the pyramids via secret passageways known only to the high-priests. Upon entry, certain rituals must be performed to allow the pyramid energy to flow through the body. Invisibility was accomplished until the sun rose in the morning.

THE EXTRAORDINARY POWERS OF TOMAS GREEN CONTINHO

Bill Cox's book **Unseen Kingdoms** gives us a glimpse of a man who is a super levitator, super alchemist and super spaceman. His name is Tomas Green Coutinho and his home is in Tres Corazones, Brazil. He is able to levitate chairs even if they are nailed to the floor. Cox saw him pick up a fork between his thumb and forefinger — then watched it double over, break, and fall to the floor in droplets of metal, as though it had been subjected to intense heat.

Transmutation (alchemy) is no problem for Tomas. He can change buttons into coins. Not only that, he can change the button into any kind of coin you ask for. Tomas has transmuted a $20 (Brazilian cruzeiros) bill into butter, and then change d it back again.

Tomas Coutinho has followers, but most of them are UFOs. A photograph of this amazing man will invariably show UFOs in the background of the picture. What's more, the ships are in focus and quite clear. One might see a mother ship with smaller craft coming out of her belly.

Bill Cox wrote an extensive article about Tomas for *The UFO Review* titled "Spaceman Show Us Your Powers." In it, Cox wrote: "Claims made by others for Tomas' extraordinary powers include the following: That he welds metals together or separates fused metals with mind power alone; charges all types of batteries applying the same phenomenal powers; transforms cotton into metal, and vice-versa; turns ashes into money, even enlarging or diminishing the object in size as he performs the mental act, and then turns the transmuted artifact back into its original state again, never touching the object, and achieving this feat while the specimen is even held in the hands of the astounded subject; and other unbelievable demonstrations."

Bill Cox tells an amusing story about a man who attended group meetings held by Tomas. Tomas performed his phenomenal acts for the group, but the man said he could no longer come to the meetings because his wife was not convinced of Tomas' powers. Tomas invited her to see for herself. She refused, saying: "If Tomas can truly bend metal with his mind, let him come here to our house, where I can control the conditions and stop the fakery."

The young man explained to Tomas that he was in a dilemma. Would he come to his house? If Tomas did not come, then it was likely that the young man would not be able to attend any of the meetings.

LEVITATION AND INVISIBILITY

Tomas was silent for awhile, then thrust his right hand forward and cried, "Hah!" He said to the young man, "It's OK now. Don't worry, she won't be a problem."

The man didn't know what he was talking about until he went home. His wife met him at the door holding a twisted fork. In stony silence she motioned for him to follow her, which he did. Then he saw that in all of the open drawers there were bent and twisted silverware and household utensils. The wife from then on was a true believer and even attended meetings.

Bill Cox said that Tomas could sharpen dull cutlery with intense mind focus. The pharmacist, in his mid-thirties, could also drive a car blindfolded on a winding mountain road. He was able to engage or disengage the moving parts of a car at will, without touching them. Once, Tomas made a quick, right-hand maneuver with the steering wheel while in traffic, yet the car continued on straight forward as though the wheel had been tightly held. At another time, while under strict laboratory conditions, Tomas placed an unoccupied car through several highway maneuvers, starting, stopping, turning and braking the car solely with the power of his mind.

Photograph taken in 1964 by Jim Templeton of his five-year-old daughter Elizabeth. The figure in background, referred to as "a spaceman," had not been present when the photograph was taken.

CHAPTER SEVEN
STRANGE, EERIE AND PECULIAR TALENTS

Levitation can be defined as the paranormal suspension of the human body in midair. For example, "simple" levitations are instances in which a Saint or holy man will become buoyant and will suddenly float up into the air, usually against his will.

Accounts also describe the "spiritual flights" of levitating mystics and yogis who, after becoming airborne, have found themselves flying through the sky. There are also cases on record of deliberately induced levitation, a phenomenon often produced by yogis.

Newton's law of gravity does not always work. There are some humans who defy the law without meaning to. They apparently have no control over themselves and will float skyward without expending any effort. Madame Alexandra David-Neal, the French explorer who spent 14 years in Tibet, relates a strange case in her book, *Mystere et magique en Tibet*.

She wrote that she had once seen a naked man weighed down with heavy chains. A friend of his told the author that because of intense mystical training, his body had become so light that if he didn't drape himself in chains he would float away.

Stories about human levitation are not rare. It is perhaps the most commonly mentioned miracle in yogic and Tibetan Buddhist Literature and in the lore of the Roman Catholic Saints. In his book, *The Wonders of the Saints*, the Reverend F. Fielding-Ould notes that:

"When we turn to the records of the Church, we find the same phenomenon observed in many instances. St. Ignatius Loyola, the founder of the Society of Jesus, was, while at prayer, seen by one John Pascal to be raised more than a foot above the ground. St. Phillip Neri was levitated 'about a palm' from his sickbed, in full view of his attendants. St. Joseph of Cupertino while celebrating the Mysteries in 1649 before the Duke of Brunswick, was bodily raised a hand's breadth above the level of the alter, and remained there six or seven minutes. St. James of Illyricum was levitated while at prayer; St. Dominic at the Holy Communion, a cubit from the ground. Much the same thing is told of St. Dunstan, St. Phillip Benite, St. Cajetan, St. Albert of Sicily, and St. Bernard Ptolomaei. St. Richard, his chancellor testifies that he saw St.

Edmund, Archbishop of Canterbury, "raised high in the air with knees bent and arms stretched out."

St. Joseph of Cupertino, who lived from 1603 to 1663, reportedly had little control over his levitations. Every time he became excited he would drift off the ground. Some say that this simple peasant from Apulia, Italy, was feeble-minded. Nevertheless, even as a youngster he tried desperately to reach religious ecstasy by whipping himself, starvation, and by wearing hair shirts. At the age of 22 he became a Franciscan monk.

It was then that the levitations grew more and more frequent. During Mass on a Sunday he rose out of his pew and flew to the alter where many candles were burning. Some of them burned Joseph quite seriously. After that episode he was no longer permitted to take part in public services.

However, the levitations continued. One day while walking with a Benedictine monk he became excited and flew up into a tree. Unfortunately, he could not fly back down again; someone had to get a ladder and assist him back down to the ground.

The many witnesses to St. Joseph's levitations were two cardinals, a surgeon, and Pope Urban VIII. He spent his entire life in prayer and was canonized because the Church felt that his levitations had to be the work of God.

THE REAL FLYING NUN

Her name was St. Teresa of Avila. She died in 1582. She was another holy person who levitated involuntarily. She wrote: "It seemed to me, when I tried to make some resistance, as if a great force beneath my feet lifted me up...I confess that it threw me into great fear, very great indeed at first; for in seeing one's body thus lifted up from the earth, though the spirit draws it upwards after itself (and that with great sweetness, if unresisted) the senses are not lost; at least I was so much myself as able to see that I was being lifted up. After the rapture was over, I have to say my body seemed frequently to be buoyant, as if all weight had departed form it, so much so that now and then I scarce knew my feet touched the ground."

St. Teresa often felt an "attack" coming on. At such times she would ask the sisters to hold her down. However, there were too many occasions when no one was nearby, and so the woman soared through the air.

St. Teresa, the famous reformer of the Carmelite order, talked also of rapture. "During rapture, the soul does not seem to animate the body. . .A rapture is absolutely irresistible, whilst union, inasmuch as we are still as on our own ground, may be hindered, though that resistance be painful and violent; it is, however, almost always impossible. But rapture, for the most part, is irresistible. It comes, in general, as a shock, quick and sharp, before you can collect your thoughts or help yourself in any way, and you see and feel it as a cloud or a strong eagle rising upwards and carrying you away on its wings."

The Saint's most famous levitation occurred during a conversation with St. John of the Cross, who had come to the convent of the Incarnation to visit her. While John spoke of the Trinity, St. Teresa knelt in prayer. Suddenly, John was rapt in ecstasy. He rose from the floor, taking his chair with him. St. Teresa was also lifted into the air. This is one of the few cases of double levitations ever recorded.

Sister Anne was another eyewitness to one of St. Teresa's levitations. She made her deposition thirty years after St. Teresa's death. The occasion was an inquiry at Segovia. Sister Anne, under oath, stated:

"On another occasion, between one and two o'clock in the daytime, I was in the choir waiting for the bell to ring, when our Holy Mother entered and knelt down for perhaps the half of a quarter of an hour. As I was looking on, she was raised about half a yard from the ground without her feet touching it. At this I was terrified, and she, for her part, was trembling all over. So I moved to where she was, and I put my hands under her feet, over which I remained weeping for something like a half an hour while the ecstasy lasted. Then suddenly she sank down and rested on her feet, and turning to me, she asked who I was, and ordered me under obedience to say nothing of what I had seen, and I have, in fact, said nothing until the present moment."

Rabi'a al-Adawiyya al-Qaysiyya was born and lived in the town of Basra, in present-day Iraq. We know little of her actual life. She apparently was born into a poor family, orphaned at a young age, separated from her sisters, and sold into slavery. Her master, perceiving her special qualities, set her free - whereupon she devoted herself, with uncompromising dedication, to the highest spiritual development. She was offered money, houses, and marriage proposals. Yet she chose to remain single and live a simple, humble life. She became famous during her life as a saint, and quickly became regarded as one of the major saints of Islam and foremost figures of the Sufi tradition.

The little that we know of Rabi'a takes the form of stories of her interactions with other people - stories that have been passed down through generations of Sufi writers. A small body of poetical prose is also attributed to her. One of the best-known stories about Rabi'a centers on an interaction with Hasan of Basra, a well-known religious leader of the time. A humorous story, it tells how Hasan tried to exploit Rabi'a's special powers for his own glory:

LEVITATION AND INVISIBILITY

One day Hasan saw Rabi'a among a group of people near the riverside. Approaching her, Hasan threw his prayer rug on the surface of the water and said, "Rabi'a, come and let us pray together here." He did this in order to display his mastery over the element of water. "Hasan," Rabi'a replied, "When you display your spiritual goods in this worldly market, you should display things that your fellow men are incapable of displaying." Then she threw her prayer rug into the air and flew up to it. "Come up here, Hasan, where people can see us!" she called. Unable to do so, Hasan said nothing. "Hasan," Rabi'a said, wishing to comfort him, "do you need to use a spiritual gift to gain a worldly reputation? What you can do, fish can also do, and what I can do, flies can also do. The real work lies beyond both of these. We should devote ourselves to the real work."

THE STRANGE POSSESSION OF FRANCOIS FONTAINE

Records show that not all levitations are performed by Saints and other holy men, but can also be demonic in origin. Sulpitius Severus described his observations of St. Martin when he approached a person possessed by unholy beings. Severus said, "The demoniac raised from the earth and remained suspended in the air, with his arms stretched out, without touching the ground with his feet... You could see the wretched person whirled about in different ways, uplifted and floated in the air with feet upwards"

An even stranger case occurred in Louviers, France, in 1591. The incident was recorded in an official report which is in the Bibliotheque Nationale of Paris. It concerns the possession of a girl named Francois Fontaine. The report reads:

"And having entered the court, the door of which is under the porch and in the passage of the prison, Francois walked but six paces into the court, and we together with our clerk entered the office where the judge's chair is and the sitting is held, and, as our clerk was beginning to writhe the present report that we were dictating to him, he cried out and showed us Francois, who was near the door of the court, whom we all saw raised about two feet off the floor, upright, and at once she fell down on the ground, flat on the back, with her arms spread out crosswise, and afterwards she was dragged, with her head foremost, still on her back, along the court, without anybody touching her or standing near her, as witnessed La Prime, the jailer, Nicolas Pellet, servant of the jailer, his wife and several prisoners who came into the court, a thing which amazed us much."

In an attempt to exorcise the demon in the girl, the Provost read the Gospel of St. John. The girl was on the floor stretched out on her back. Suddenly, she raised up, horizontally, for about three or four feet, and was carried by some unseen force toward the exorcist, who fled to his office in terror.

The report states: ". . .as we continued to read the Gospel of St. John, the body of Francois, who was then lying on the ground, face upwards, began to crawl along, head foremost, all disheveled and bristly, and all at once the body of Francois was raised off the floor, three or four feet high, and borne horizontally, face upwards along the court, without anything to support her. When we saw the body make straight for us, thus suspended in midair, it threw us into such a fright that we withdrew into the office of the court, locking the door behind us and reading the Gospel of St. John down to the end.

"But the body kept following us through the air up to the office, against the door of which it struck with the soles of its feet, and then was carried back through the air, with the face upwards and head foremost, out of the court. This gave such a fright to the jailer, her servants, our archers and many prisoners who were present with several inhabitants of Louviers, that they fled, some into the prison, some into the street, after shutting the doors behind them; and the body of Francois was carried away out of the court and remained in the passage of the prison, between the door of it and the street door which the fugitives had shut in their flight. We considered this with great astonishment, till one Desjardins and other prisoners opened the door of the prison and said they would help us, which enabled us to get out of the office and court, having thus found Francois lying on the ground close to the prison door."

Later on an attempt was made to give her the Holy Sacrament as a means of chasing the demon away. It didn't work. The demon's power was mightier than the exorcist. The report says: "And Francois, kneeling down, had been most alarmingly carried away, without being able to take the Sacrament, opening her mouth, rolling her eyes in her head in such a horrible way that it had been necessary, with the help of five of six persons, to pull her down by her dress as she was raised into the air, and they had thrown her down on the floor . . .Then the cure had presented the Holy Host again to Francois, who had knelt down; but she was again snatched off the floor, higher than the alter, as if she had been taken by the hair, in such a strange way that the bystanders were much amazed, and would never have thought of witnessing so frightful a thing, and they all knelt and began saying prayers. . ."

The cure Pellet made still another attempt to give the girl Holy Communion, and "she had been for the third time prevented from taking it, having been for the third time carried over a large bench that was before the alter where Mass was said, and lifted up into the air towards where a glass had been broken, with her head downwards and her feet upwards, without her clothes being upset, through which, before and behind, was belching forth much water and stinking smoke. . .and for some time thus carried through the air, till at last seven or eight men had taken hold of her and brought her down to the ground."

The report does not tell us what eventually happened to Francois Fontaine. We can only hope that the demon left her body and that she returned to a normal life. What the story does tell, however, is that the power of levitation is not exclusive to Saints and other holy people. The power could be dormant in all of us, needing only the proper catalyst to set it into action.

St. Joseph of Cupertino

CHAPTER EIGHT
THE ENIGMA OF D.D. HOME

D.D. Home was a Spiritualist born in Scotland in 1833 and was brought up in America. As a child he was sickly and possibly suffered from attacks of hysteria. The first hint of his psychic ability came when he was 13. He had a vision of his friend, Edwin. He told his family that Edwin had been dead for three days. Home was right. News came that Edwin had died three days earlier.

Home's psychic powers developed through his teen years. Before he died at the age of 53, he was noted for being able to perform three types of miracles: He was able to handle fire without burning himself, levitate at will, and to move heavy objects without touching them physically.

Home was 34 in 1867 when he met young Lord Adare, a British correspondent for the Daily Telegraph. There were several other witnesses in the room when Home stirred the embers in the fireplace with his hands, keeping both hands in the flames until the embers caught. He then placed his face in the glowing embers, moving it about as though bathing it in water. His flesh was examined by witnesses, but no one could find any evidence of charring. Later that night Home held a glowing ember in his hands for several minutes. It was so hot that no one else could come close to it.

Home rubbed elbows with the great figures of the day, Napoleon III, the Empress Eugenie, Count Alexis Tolstoy, Elizabeth Barrett Browning and William Makepeace Thackeray. Thomas Trollope, brother of the novelist Anthony, decided to check up on Home by talking to the most famous stage magician of the period, Bartolomeo Bosco. Bosco said that there was absolutely no trickery that he could see in Home's performance. No mere conjurer could match Home's miracles. The amazing miracles were never performed on a stage. Home preferred someone's parlor, and he liked to have influential people as witnesses. Nor did he ever accept money for his work.

HOME'S FEATS OF LEVITATION

On scores of occasions Home rose straight up into the air and floated about the room to the amazement of guests. Often, these witnesses would pass their hands around him while he was suspended in mid-air. He once rose so high that he made a chalk mark on the ceiling.

One guest on this occasion was a skeptical reporter named F.L. Burr, editor of *the Hartford Times*. He wrote later:

"Suddenly, without any expectation on the part of the company, Home was taken up into the air. I had hold of his hand at the time and I felt his feet. . .they were lifted a foot from the floor. He palpitated from head to foot with the contending emotions of joy and fear which choked his utterances. Again and again he was taken from the floor, and the third time he was carried to the ceiling of the apartment, with which his hands and feet came into gentle contact."

Home's most famous feat of levitation occurred on December 16, 1868. Three reputable witnesses were present when this extraordinary event took place, Lord Adare, the Master of Lindsay, and Captain Wynne. All of them watched in astonishment as D. D Home floated into the air, went out one window and floated back into another. The windows of the fashionable London home were 80 feet high.

Home had conducted more than 1,500 séances and had never been detected as a fraud. However, this business of floating out of one window and back into another was hard for most people to believe. Suspicion arouse when it was learned that Home insisted that his three witnesses remain seated until he re-emerged through the window. Being English gentlemen, they obeyed. What would they have seen, however, had they rushed to the window and looked out? Would they have seen Home walking a tightrope, or swinging by a rope to the other window? The answer will never be known.

The three witnesses were convinced that true Levitation had occurred. Lord Adare wrote in a book devoted to Home: "Presently Home appeared, standing upright, outside our window. He opened the window and came in quite coolly. I went with him into the next room. The window was not raised a foot...He then went out through the space; head first, his body being horizontal and apparently rigid. Amazingly, he came in once again, feet foremost."

The Master of Lindsay said: "We heard the window in the next room lifted up, and almost immediately after saw Home floating in the air outside our window. He remained in this position a few seconds, then raised the window and glided into the room, feet foremost, and sat down."

In a letter to Home, the third witness, Captain Charles Wynne, said: "I don't think anyone who knows me would for a moment say I was a victim to hallucination or any other humbug of the kind. The fact of your having gone out of the window and in the other, I can swear to."

LEVITATION AND INVISIBILITY

D.D. Home once accomplished a Houdini-like feat that would have made the great escape artist envious. The incident was reported by Mr. Sergeant Cox, a respected member of the bar. Cox was in the room with chemist Sir William Crookes; his brother, Walter, and famed ethnologist and traveler E. Galton.

These four men were the testers. They tied Home to a chair with tightly wound copper wire. The psychic's wrist and ankles were bound. The chair was then wired to an iron gate and all the joints were soldered. A dressing gown was placed on top and the sleeves were sewn together. The windows and doors to the room were locked. Home could not move any part of his body.

The testers moved to the next room, which was separated by an archway and a curtain. This room was fully lighted with gas burners. Four minutes of silence followed. Then a bell in Home's room was rung. A chair, a footstool and other pieces of furniture were pushed through the curtain.

Sergeant Cox wrote: "Presently, the curtains were partially drawn, and there was a man, dressed like a sailor, but whose features were exactly like those of Home. We were all satisfied it was indeed Home. He stood there talking to us for half an hour, answering questions. I said, 'Are you substantial or only a shape?' 'I am as solid as you are,' was the answer. Then he said, 'Will you thrust your finger in my mouth?' He opened his jaws and I thrust in my finger. He gave me a bite that made me cry. Having held me thus for nearly a minute, he let go, and with a loud laugh said,' Do you call that psychic force?'"

The four men then went through the curtain. Cox wrote: "The psychic (Home) was as we left him, only in a state of unconsciousness. The wires were uncut, the solder perfect, the chair bound to the gate, the dressing gown upon him. The door was locked, the seals upon it and the window unbroken. He was wearing the dress suit in which we had tied him up."

Apparently, Daniel Dunglas Home was able to communicate with the dead. When his fame spread throughout London he was invited into homes at the rate of six or seven times a week, conducting séances to amuse and startle his followers. For that service he was fed, clothed and kept in pocket money. The wealthy and influential adored him.

DISCIPLE OF EVIL?

Eventually, Homes set his sights on Europe, and gained more conquests. In 1855 he went to Florence, Italy, and was the guest of the mother of novelist Anthony Trolope. From there he went to Naples and stayed with a noble Polish family. In Rome, he wanted desperately to become a Catholic. However, here he ran into a snag. The Church knew all about D.D. Home. It did not think he made a good subject for conversion. The chief of the inquisition made him sign a document which read:

"I Daniel Dunglas Home, hereby solemnly declare and avow that I have not sold my soul to the Devil, nor have I on any occasion been cognizant of holding communications with the Evil One. — Rome, March 18, 1856."

The following year the urge to embrace Catholicism may have faded. He was now holding séances for the Emperor Napoleon III and his Empress Eugenie. He permitted them to touch spirit hands. Home also materialized the hand of Napoleon Bonaparte, which grabbed a pencil and scrawled his signature. Later it was verified as being his.

Palace gates were opened to him. Home walked the huge rooms of mansions belonging to great financiers. Witnesses claimed his mediumship was something to behold. When Home went into a trance, musical instruments played, floating in the air. Bells rang. Solid objects appeared from nowhere. Tables rose off the floor. D.D. Home was able to stretch his body from three to five inches, to the astonishment of doctors and scientists. He could also shrink himself by as many inches.

On another trip to Rome, he fell in love with a wealthy Russian girl. Twelve days later they were engaged, but the Czar had to give his approval. For Home, that was no problem. He went to Peterhof Palace and dazzled the Czar with his occult powers. Consent was given, along with a large diamond ring. Another ring was given by the Czar when the couple's baby was born.

Unfortunately things started going wrong for Home. In 1864 the Church of Rome branded him as a disciple of the devil. He was, the Church stated, a sorcerer. Home had to leave Rome in a hurry. Then his wife died. Her family tightened the reins on the family fortune and it was necessary for the psychic to sue. The suit was settled in his favor. However, that was followed by another suit, this one from the woman who had adopted him as her son. Over the years she had given him gifts valued at sixty thousand pounds. Now she wanted them back, and she won her case in court.

Undaunted, Home went to Russia, where he found a wealthy woman willing to marry him. He spent years in Russia, amusing his hosts and hostesses in wealthy and fashionable homes.

Back in England in 1870, Home was in trouble. There was a popular clamor for an investigation of this man who could levitate and speak to the dead. The one chosen to do the job was Sir William Crookes, a brilliant chemist and physicist. Crookes was the inventor of the x-ray tube which still bears his name today. To do the job properly, Crookes used a great deal of apparatus, much of it designed especially for the experiments. He wrote about his results in the July 1, 1871 issue of the *Quarterly Journal of Science*. In his article,

LEVITATION AND INVISIBILITY

Crookes stated that under conditions of perfect control, Home had floated in the air supported by an unknown force. He had handled red hot coals without injury, and objects near Home had moved by themselves.

Tragically, that report dogged Crookes to his grave. He was stigmatized as having been a fool and a dupe. Still, he refused to change his mind. Twenty years later he wrote: "I find nothing to retract or to alter. I have discovered no flaw in the experiments then made, or in the reasoning I based on them."

D.D. Home died at Auteuil near Paris in 1886. For some thirty years he had lived a life of ease, doing nothing more strenuous than holding séances. The tragedy is that he might have taken his mediumship to great heights if he had chosen to do something other than entertain the wealthy.

Many times Home was seen to rise straight up into the air and float about the room to the amazement of guests. Often, these witnesses would pass their hands around him while he was suspended in mid-air. He once rose so high that he made a chalk mark on the ceiling.

CHAPTER NINE
NOW YOU CAN LEARN THE ART OF LEVITATION

Unknown to most people is the fact that just about anyone can levitate. You don't have to be a psychic. You don't have to have some kind of magical formula. All you have to know is the rules of levitation, and be willing to obey them.

Students of transcendental meditation are taught to levitate under the supervision of Maharishi Mahesh Yogi at his headquarters in Switzerland. On student described the experience this way: "People would rock gently, then more and more, then start lifting off into the air. You should really be in a lotus position to do it, you can hurt yourself landing if you've got a dangling undercarriage. To begin with it's like the Wright brothers' first flight, you come down with a bump. That's why we have to sit on foam rubber cushions. Then you learn to control it better, and it becomes totally exhilarating."

His Holiness Maharishi Mahesh offered his opinion on the human potential for levitation: "Yoga means union, the union of the individual awareness with the Unified Field of all the Laws of Nature in the state of Transcendental Consciousness. 'Yogic flying' demonstrates the ability of the individual to act from the Unified Field and enliven the total potential of Natural Law in all its expressions - mind, body, behavior, and environment. 'Yogic flying' presents in miniature the flight of galaxies in space, all unified in perfect order by natural law.

"The mind-body coordination displayed by 'Yogic Flying' shows that consciousness and its expression - the physiology- is in perfect balance. Scientific research has found maximum coherence in human brain functioning during 'Yogic Flying'. As the coherently functioning human brain is the unit of world peace, 'Yogic Flying' is the mechanics to make world peace a reality, and thereby bring world health, world happiness, world prosperity, a world free from suffering, heaven on earth in this generation."

THE THREE STAGES OF YOGIC FLYING

According to the ancient Vedic texts, Yogic Flying develops in three stages, each representing a more refined style of physiological functioning. In the first stage, the body rises into the air in a series of short hops. This rising of the body involves no physical effort but merely a faint intention deep within the mind.

Even in its first state, the hopping stage, the practice of Yogic Flying creates waves of bubbling bliss in the consciousness and physiology of the practitioner. The mind-body coordination displayed by Yogic Flying shows that consciousness and its expression, the physiology, are in perfect balance. Scientific Research has found that there is maximum coherence in brain waves during Yogic Flying indicating highly orderly and holistic functioning of the brain.

In the second stage of Yogic Flying, the body rises into the air and remains there, floating. A number of Yogic Flyers have reported that they have risen into the air and remained there for a discernible moment before coming back down. In the third and final stage of Yogic Flying, the body flies through the air at will.

TM students insist that the only way to true weightlessness is through stringent mental training. Both physical and spiritual discipline is needed, they say. However, the feat is being accomplished countless times in homes, school yards, and in bars all over the world.

The phenomenon is simple to execute. The one to be levitated sits in a chair. Four people stand around him and place their index fingers in his armpits and in the crooks of his knees. Then they place their hands in a pile above his head, making sure that no one person's two hands are touching. The hands are interwoven. All four persons then concentrate deeply for about fifteen seconds. At a signal, the hands are then returned to the armpits and crooks of the knees of the subject, making sure that only the index fingers are used. At the count of three the subject can be easily lifted from the chair and into the air.

The person who is being levitated should not do anything to cooperate or resist. He should not become active in any way. The four standing persons should work in rhythm. Each participant should know what he has to do, and when he has to do it.

For instance, person Number One, standing at the seated person's right, should place his right hand on top of the seated person's head. Person Number Two, at right rear, places his right hand on top of Person Number One's right hand. Person Number Three, left rear, places his right hand on top of Person Number Two's right hand. Person Number Four places his right hand on top of the others. There are no four hands on top of one another. The process is now repeated, starting with Person Number One placing his left hand on top and continuing until all eight hands are in place. The movements should be practiced until everyone is in rhythm and there is an easy flow.

LEVITATION AND INVISIBILITY

After the fifteen seconds of concentration, and when the person timing the event calls out, "Lift!" All four participants must place their forefingers as follows: Person one places his forefingers under the right knee of the seated subject. Person two places his forefingers under the right armpit. Person three places his fingers under the left armpit, and person four under the left knee. These movements should also be practiced until they are smooth and effortless.

Usually, there is a lot of giggling and laughing because the idea seems so absurd. However, it has been shown that after three or four attempts, when the chuckling has died down, there will usually be a measure of success. If done properly, it is actually possible to "lift" an individual by the use of just several fingers placed at specific pressure points on the body of the person to be levitated.

Rhythm is important. So is practice. One Parapsychologist told me that he conducts the experiment in class quite frequently and has met with failure only once. In most cases the person who is levitated is raised about two to four feet in the air and experiences a feeling of lightness and exhilaration.

My friend also told me that after a lot of practice, it is no longer necessary to place four pairs of hands on top of the seated person's head. It seems that all that is necessary is for the four people to chant a phrase in unison five or six times. Any phrase will do. He said that "apple pie" is a good one. So is "vanilla sundae." Almost any innocuous phrase will do. The parapsychologist did emphasize that rhythm is extremely important. Levitation without it is impossible. If you do it with rhythm, there is little sensation of energy being expended.

According to the parapsychologist I spoke to, documentation on actual cases of levitation are rare, and that is because most of the claims are anecdotal and therefore not acceptable in scientific circles.

What that means is that there are a lot of stories, but no real proof. We mentioned earlier that Christ walked on water that St. Joseph of Cupertino levitated, once as high as the topmost spires of St. Peter's Cathedral with hundreds watching. St. Teresa and St. John of the Cross levitated together right up to the ceiling. The scientists say that these are merely stories, and that all religions have them.

Some scientists are likely to make light of the subject by relating a Zen tale in which a disciple left his teacher to spend many years in solitary meditation. On his return, his guru asked him what he had learned with his years of meditation. The disciple said proudly that he had learned to walk across the river on top of the water, to which the guru replied, "A pity. For one rupee the ferry will carry you across."

LEVITATION AND INVISIBILITY

AN INDIAN YOGI LEVITATES WITH 150 WITNESSES

The date was June 6, 1936. The story and photos appeared in the *Illustrated London News*. The Indian yogi was Subbayah Pullavar. A witness, P.Y. Plunkett, stated: "The time was about 12:30PM and the sun directly above us so that shadows played no part in the performance. Standing quietly by was Subbayah Pullavar, the performer, with long hair, a drooping mustache and a wild look in his eye. He salaamed to us and stood chatting for awhile. He had been practicing this particular branch of yoga for nearly twenty years."

About 150 witnesses gathered about the performer. He began his ritual. Water was poured around the tent in which he was to levitate. Shoes with leather soles were banned inside the circle of water. The yogi entered the tent alone. Moments later aids removed the tent and there was the fakir suspended in the air about 36 inches from the ground. He held on to a cloth covered stick, but lightly and apparently only for balance and not for support. The manner in which he held the stick indicated that no exertion at all was being used. The space around and under the yogi was examined thoroughly, but the investigators could find no strings or any kind of invisible apparatus. The yogi was in a trance state. Photographs were taken from various angles during the four minutes the Indian was levitated.

Plunkett said that the tent was erected again so that the yogi could descend in private. However, Plunkett said he managed to witness it. "After about a minute," the witness said, "he appeared to away and then very slowly began to descend, still in a horizontal position. He took about five minutes to move from the top of the stick to the ground, a distance of about three feet. When Subbayah was back on the ground his assistants carried him over to where we were sitting and asked if we would try to bend his limbs. Even with assistance we were unable to do so." The Indian had to be splashed with water and rubbed for five minutes before he came around and was able to use his limbs.

A YOGI'S DESCRIPTION OF HIS LEVITATION EXPERIENCE

From ***Autobiography of a Yogi,*** by Paramhansa Yogananda, Pgs. 320 and 321. After I had finished writing this chapter, I sat on my bed in the lotus posture. My room was dimly lit by two shaded lamps. Lifting my gaze, I noticed that the ceiling was dotted with small mustard-colored lights, scintillating and quivering with a radium like luster. Myriads of penciled rays, like sheets of rain, gathered into a transparent shaft and poured silently upon me.

At once my physical body lost its grossness and became metamorphosed into astral texture. I felt a floating sensation as, barely touching the bed, the weightless body shifted slightly and alternatively to left and right. I looked around the room; the furniture and walls were as usual, but the little mass of light had so multiplied that the ceiling was all but invisible. I was wonderstruck.

"This is the cosmic motion-picture mechanism." A Voice spoke as though from within the light. "Shedding its beam on the white screen of your bed sheets, it is producing the picture of your body. Behold, your form is nothing but light!"

I gazed at my arms and moved them back and forth, yet could not feel their weight. Ecstatic joy overwhelmed me. The cosmic stem of light, blossoming as my body, seemed a divine reproduction of the light beams that stream out of the projection booth in a cinema house and make manifest the pictures on the screen.

For a long time I experienced this motion picture of my body in the faintly lit theater of my own bedroom. Though I have has many visions, none was ever more singular. As the illusion of a solid body was completely dissipated, and as my realization deepened that the essence of all objects is light, I looked up to the throbbing stream of lifetrons and spoke entreatingly.

"Divine Light, please withdrew this, my humble bodily picture, into Thyself; even as Elijah was drawn up to the heaven in a chariot of flame."

This prayer was evidently startling; the beam disappeared. My body resumed its normal weight and sank on the bed ; the swarm of dazzling ceiling lights flickered and vanished. My time to leave this earth had apparently not arrived.

Also from *Autobiography of a Yogi* pgs. 323 and 324. In an interview with the one Yogananda calls Sacred Mother. She had been the wife of his guru's guru. Her name is Kashi Moni. He asked her for a few stories from her life.

"It was years before I came to realize the divine stature of my husband," she began. "One night, in this very room, I had a vivid dream. Glorious angels floated in unimaginable grace above me. So realistic was the sight that I awoke at once; strangely, the room was enveloped in a dazzling light. My husband, in the lotus posture, was levitated in the center of the room, surrounded by angels. In supplicating dignity they were worshiping him with palm-folded hands.

"Astonished beyond measure, I was convinced that I was still dreaming.

"'Woman,' Lahiri Mahasaya said, 'you aren't dreaming. Forsake your sleep forever and ever.' As he slowly descended to the floor, I prostrated myself at this feet.

LEVITATION AND INVISIBILITY

THE BATCHELDOR REPORT

I've found that most parapsychologists believe that levitation is possible under controlled conditions. One experiment, apparently has truly achieved levitation. Written up in the September 1966 issue of *the Journal of the Society for Psychical Research*, the article was entitled: "Report on a Case of Table Levitation and Associated Phenomena."

The author, British psychologist K. J. Batcheldor, says that he does not expect scientists to accept what he says at face value, but that he would be content if he succeeds in "inducing some few of my readers to suspend disbelief long enough to attempt sustained experimentations for themselves."

He means you and me. I've tried it, and it works exactly as Batheldor dictates. It can be done. Here's your chance to see how good you are.

LEVITATING A TABLE

Batcheldor learned that Tomas Faraday, the electrical wizard, had already known in 1853, that if a group of people sit at a table with their hands resting on its surface, the combined unconscious muscular action of the sitters can make the table tilt and dance. However, Batcheldor and his assistants were in for a surprise when they sat at a table in the spirit of amusement. He said the attitude "changed sharply in the eleventh meeting, when the table, instead of merely tilting or rocking on two legs, as it had done so far, rose clear from the floor. The explanation of unconscious muscle action was suddenly no longer applicable, since one cannot push a table up into the air, either consciously or unconsciously, when the hands are on top of it."

Batcheldor conducted 200 sittings in more than 18 months. He noted that in 80 of these sittings he was successful, and that in each case one of the sitters was a man named W. G. Chick. The phenomenon occurred only when Chick was at the table.

In my discussions with parapsychologists on this subject, I learned that they found the same truth in their experiments. One person, a medium or a sensitive, has the power to raise the table. If he or she is at the table, it will likely rise.

Batcheldor had another problem. The Early sittings were done in darkness, a fact which would have been pounded upon by skeptics. After the first levitation the table was equipped as follows:

"Four switches, one on each foot, were joined in a series to a battery lamp. The red lamp would light if, and only if, all four legs came off the floor. The apparatus stood up extremely well to the rough treatment it received during the more violent motions of the table, and a most vigorous deliberate rocking and tilting would not give a false signal."

The apparatus was used on tables ranging from two pounds to forty pounds. Batcheldor writes of the twelfth sitting when the apparatus was attached to a fifteen- pound table: "This twelfth meeting proved to be extremely colorful, containing the largest number of total levitations ever witnessed in one sitting. At first the table seemed to 'try out' the device 'tentatively' (it is difficult to resist such anthropomorphism). Gradually the movements became bolder and the lamp was lit for longer periods. By its red glow we could clearly see our hands on top of the table. The table then seemed to act as an excited person would, and proceeded to execute all manner of very lively movements rocking, swaying, jumping, dancing, tilting, oscillating bodily both slowly and rapidly; it shook like a live thing even when totally levitated, almost shaking our hands off."

At this point in the amazing experiment, Batcheldor wanted to find out what the response would be if he issued vocal commands. He says: "Because the levitations were not very high, I said: 'Come on — higher!' At which the table rose up chest high and remained there for eight seconds. . .At one point the table levitated and floated right across the room. We had to leave our seats to follow it; it appeared to be about five inches off the floor, and the signal lamp remained alight until we crashed into some other furniture near the wall and the table dropped to the floor. When we reseated ourselves in the center of the room, the table soon came to life again, and took to rising up and then banging itself down with tremendous force, so that we feared it would break."

You might want to try this experiment with a group of friends. It's suggested that you use a light-weight table, like a bridge table, and insist that the group concentrate on levitating the table. The group should sit around the table and place their fingertips lightly on the surface of the table. Much like you would the pointer on a Ouija board.

It usually takes about ten to fifteen minutes of concentration before the table will start to respond. Sometimes it takes several sessions before any effect is noticed. It must be pointed out, however, that a dancing table, or tilting table, is not true levitation. It must rise off the floor with all four legs suspended in the air. A table that simply dances can be the result of unconscious muscular action in the hands.

LEVITATION AND INVISIBILITY

Japanese yoga master MASAHARU NARUSE, known also as AKASHA GIRI, demonstrates his levitation technique by using prana, or vital energy that permeates the universe.

CHAPTER TEN
IS LEVITATION USEFUL?

Some experts feel that true levitation is associated only with those who are deeply religious. Nearly all sects can describe certain members who enjoyed the phenomenon. Aleister Crowley met a friend named Alan Bennett in 1902. Bennett had become a Buddhist monk and had become so weightless that he was blown about like leaf.

The French explorer, Alexandra David-Neel, tells of seeing a long-distance running by a Tibetan lama during the early part of the 20th Century. The explorer said that the Lama seemed to lift himself off the ground proceeding by leaps. It was as though he had been endowed with the elasticity of a ball and rebounded each time his feet touched the ground. He ran with the regularity of a pendulum. He is said to have run hundreds of miles using this strange form of locomotion, keeping his eyes fixed on some far-distant goal.

Nijinsky, the famed Russian ballet dancer, also had the unique ability of appearing to be almost weightless. He would leap high and fall slowly, like a feather, in what was known as the slow vault. His biographer, Cyril W. Beaumont, describes his dancing thus, "That wonderful leap by which, as the sprite in The Spectre of the Rose he entered through the open French windows to alight beside the sleeping girl, must still linger in the memories of all who saw it. There was no flurry, no strained features, no thud as the feet came to the ground; it was just as though a rose petal had been caught up by a night breeze and wafted through the open window."

Nijinsky claimed he could stay up as long as he wished, and come down when he felt like it

The noted fortean writer John Keel in his book, ***Jadoo*** (Gilbert Press), told about his strange meeting in Tibet with a timid little lama named Nyang-Pas. Keel had heard that Nyang-Pas was a great Siddha, someone who can perform miracles. The lama however, denied it. "I am just a simple lama, I only practice the teachings of my religion."

When Keel asked Nyang-Pas if he could be taught something, the lama said: "It would take you a lifetime of solitude. . .but perhaps I can introduce you to the principle."

LEVITATION AND INVISIBILITY

John Keel takes up the story: "He struggled to his feet, pressed one hand on the top of his walking stick, a heavy branch about four feet long, frowned a little with effort, and then slowly lifted his legs up off the floor until he was sitting cross-legged in the air. There was nothing behind him or under him. His sole support was his stick, which he seemed to use to keep his balance."

"Can you teach me this?" Keel asked.

"No," came the reply, "it is not something you can learn overnight, it is a matter of will. But there are other things, basic things, for example, think of an object, some common thing."

Keel thought of a tree, the lama gazed deep into his eyes and smiled.

"That is too easy. You are thinking of a tree, try something else."

Next Keel thought of an old pair of boots. Again, the lama guessed correctly.

Again Keel asked to be taught the secrets, but the lama told him he would have to learn for himself with practice. His instructions were simple, first Keel had to cleanse his mind of all thoughts and concentrate entirely on his subject. If the subject is a reasonably intelligent person, able to visualize strongly the object he is thinking of, an image of that object would pop into Keels mind.

The object must be visualized. Words can't be intercepted by a novice telepath. And disciplined people tend to think in words rather than in images. As for levitation, Nyang-Pas explained that it takes a very high form of concentration, separating mental vision from the body, till the body becomes lighter then air.

AN ANCIENT ART

Research into this fascinating subject has brought us into contact with literature on the ancients, who apparently had mastered levitation to a far greater degree than we moderns. Enormous earthworks, for instance, in England and the desert patterns in Peru, had to have been accomplished by people who could levitate easily. The white horse at Uffington in Oxfordshire is carved on terrain so hilly that it can be appreciated only from the air, indicating that only levitators could have designed it.

The ancient Druids allegedly could fly at will, yet there is some feeling among the experts that they may have flown in out-of-body experiments rather than actual physical flight.

Those who have truly accomplished the art of levitation say that with few exceptions the phenomenon requires training and discipline for a long period of time. There is a mysterious law at work, a law that says the body will be given permission to defy the law of gravity.

Spontaneous or random levitations may also work on this principle. The levitator may accidentally stumble upon the natural ability that permits them to rise into the air. Investigator Charles Fort, who wrote huge volumes of strange events during the early part of this century came across a case of a 12-year old boy named Henry Jones from Shepton Mallet in England who rose to the ceiling on several occasions. The year was 1657. At one time the boy was observed sailing over a garden wall. The distance was 30 yards. If he knew the secret formula, it didn't last long for him. After one year he lost his ability to levitate. Afterwards he was shunned by the townspeople who believed him bewitched.

A FIRST HAND EXPERIENCE

"My sensation was that of being lighter than the air. No pressure on any part of the body, no unconsciousness or enhancement. From the position of the mark on the wall, it is clear that my head must have been close to the ceiling. The ascent, of which I was perfectly conscious, was very gradual and steady, not unlike that of being in a elevator, but without any perceptible sensation of motion other than that of feeling lighter than the atmosphere, of being completely free."

That is a description of how it feels to experience the phenomenon of levitation, the rising of ones physical body against the natural force of gravitation. It is particularly noteworthy because the narrator was William Stainton Moses, a most remarkable English religious figure, medium, and psychical researcher. He was one of the founding members of the British Society for Psychical Research, and a man of such unquestionable integrity that Andrew Lang, in discussing the possibility of fraud in some of Moses's phenomena, said that "the choice was between a moral and a physical miracle."

W. Stainton Moses was levitated a number of times in front of respectable witnesses. On one occasion he was swept up from his feet, thrown onto a large table and then onto an adjacent sofa. Though it seemed to the others present that a tremendous amount of force was involved, Moses suffered no injury whatsoever.

The nature of levitation suggests that the ability may draw upon the same source of energy as does poltergeist activity. We understand now that the poltergeist is a purely natural phenomenon centering around a target subject who is often a juvenile at the age of puberty, or someone experiencing great stress and mental anguish. It seems reasonable to suppose that the force emanating from the target subject, in a manner science does not fully understand, and capable of moving relatively heavy objects such as furniture could, if directed toward the ground, effectively lift that subject's body into the air.

We find levitation associated with a few poltergeist cases, though sometimes it is not the target subject who is lifted up. The classic case of the Epworth Vicarage Poltergeist is an example. Nancy Wesley, daughter of the Vicar, was often elevated in the presence of her four sisters. However, the available evidence in this case is that the target subject was sister Hetty.

It has been said that some who levitate are able to extend their power to others who hold them by the hand. This is questionable. It seems more likely that it is just impossible to overcome the levitating force. Harry Keller, the stage magician who, before Houdini's time, investigated the claims of many mediums, witnessed and inadvertently participated in a levitation of the medium William Eglinton.

Keller wrote for the Proceedings of the SPR, "I was placed on Mr. Eglinton's left and seized his left hand firmly in mine ... I felt him rise slowly in the air and as I retained firm hold of his hand, I was pulled to my feet, and subsequently compelled to jump on a chair and then on the table in order to retain my hold on him. That his body did ascend in the air on that occasion with an apparent disregard for the law of gravity, there can be no doubt." Keller added that his own body appeared to have been rendered non-susceptible to gravity as he felt the levitating effects of the medium.

There are some recorded instances when a weight loss of a levitator is immediately evident to witnesses. In Grenoble, France, a girl given to ecstatic trances became so stiff and light at times that it was possible to lift her from the ground by merely holding her elbow. A very unusual case was that of Frau Frederica Hauffe, the famous Seeress of Prevorst. According to Dr. Justinus Kerner, the man who investigated the remarkable powers that centered around her, while she was in a trance she was put into a bath where she floated like a cork to the top of the water. Dr. Kerner reported that if he placed his hand against hers, he could draw her up from the ground as if he were a magnet.

GRAVITY WAVE

At first glance, cases such as these seem to suggest that weight, as if it were a substantial, corporeal entity, had been withdrawn from the body. However, this is not the proper way to look at the situation. Weight is not such an energy, weight is the quality of a reaction. That is, weight is the reaction of a mass to the gravitational attraction of another mass. When we weigh something, we are not weighing something tangible, but rather the reaction of that thing to the gravitational pull of the Earth.

It would seem, then, that somewhere between the center of gravity of a levitator and the center of gravity of the Earth, a line of force is set up that has the effect of neutralizing the pull of gravity on all other points in the elevated body. For some years now, Dr. Joseph Weber of the University of Maryland has been experimenting with something called a gravity wave. Scientists have observed that the laws that govern electrostatic attraction, electromagnetic waves, and gravity, seem to act as if they were manifestations of some greater general law. This is the Unified Field Theory that Albert Einstein was working on at the time of his death. He sought one law that would apply to all of those similar phenomenon so that interaction between them could be studied.

It is entirely within the realm of possibility that a link may exist between the gravity wave and certain waves generated in the nervous system of the human body. Dr. Weber's work indicates the gravitational wave has a frequency of 1600 cycles per second. A wave generated at the same rate, but out of phase with the gravity wave, would neutralize it. This could produce buoyancy, but not levitation.

However, if a brain wave or a nervous system wave, out of phase with the gravity wave to the proper degree were generated, then the force of gravity would theoretically be overcome. According to this idea, electric waves generated within the levitator would oppose the force of gravity along a thin line extending between their center of gravity and that of the Earth.

The one thing that stands out in all levitation cases is that the levitator was in an altered state of consciousness. It seems clear that the ecstatic reaches levitation through meditation of an intense sort. The medium achieves something similar by deliberately going into trance. The medium Willi Schneider used to increase his breath rate to about 75 per minute to achieve trance. It is interesting that at that rate, both heartbeat and breath would probably be synchronized. Levitation then, seems to depend upon a trance or altered mental state of consciousness. Breathing exercises are apparently one means of approaching this phenomenon.

Levitation is not limited to human beings; furniture and all types of heavy objects have been levitated -although here again there may be some overlapping of function, and the levitation of material objects might come under the heading of Psychokinesis. In his ***The Psychic World Around Us,*** Long John Nebel tells of the levitation of a Hammond church organ by a psychic named William Daut. It rose slowly, gaining momentum; then after 15 or 20 seconds it stopped, suspended in mid air some 10 inches off the floor. Nebel's informants, whom he trusted implicitly, declared they examined the organ thoroughly and that there were no wires, hoists, jacks or any other mechanical means that could account for its elevation.

Abraham Lincoln, who possessed psychic powers of his own had a lifelong interest in the occult. Spiritualism was very much in vogue during that era, and Mary Todd Lincoln was fascinated by the subject; every new medium who arose on the social horizon was inevitably invited to the White House to display her talents. During one of these séances, Lincoln writes, a heavy mahogany grand piano was raised off the floor and stood suspended in mid-air.

Naturally, many theories are advanced to explain these strange happenings. One very obscure one deals with a cantilever theory accounting for the movement of distant objects by the extrusion of elastic and resisting pseudopods from the body of the medium. "The teleplastic levers have naturally their fulcrum on the floor," the theory explains.

"The force of gravity is not eluded, but simply opposed by a contrary upward force. The spent amount of energy is not above that required for the production of a fair phenomenon of telekinesis."

COULD SOUND BE A KEY TO LEVITATION?

Richard Clark, PhD gives the following explanation in a chapter he wrote for the book **Anti-Gravity and The World Grid** (Adventures Unlimited Press): "We know from the priests of the Far East that they were able to lift heavy boulders up high mountains with the help of groups of various sounds ... the knowledge of the various vibrations in the audio range demonstrates to a scientist of physics that a vibrating and condensed sound field can nullify the power of gravity.

"The following is based on observations which were made in Tibet. I have this report from civil engineer and flight manager, Henry Kjelson, a friend of mine. He later on included this in his book, The Lost Techniques. A Swedish doctor, Dr. Jarl, a friend of Kjelsons, studied at oxford. During those times he became friends with a young Tibetan student. In 1939, Dr. Jarl made a journey to Egypt for the English Scientific Society. There he was seen by a messenger of his Tibetan friend, and urgently requested to come to Tibet to meet a high Lama.

"Dr. Jarl followed the messenger and arrived after a long journey by plane and yak caravans through the mountains, at the monastery, where the old Lama and his friend who was now holding a high position were living. Dr. Jarl stayed in Tibet for some time, and because of his friendship with the Tibetans he learned a lot of things that other foreigners had no chance to hear about, or observe.

"One day his friend took him to a place in the neighborhood of the monastery and showed him a sloping meadow which was surrounded in the North West by high cliffs. In one of the rock walls, at a height of about 250 meters, was a huge hole which looked like the entrance to a cave. In front of this hole there was a platform on which the monks were building a rock wall. The only access to this platform was from the top of the cliff and the monks lowered themselves down with the help of ropes.

"In the middle of the meadow, about 250 meters from the cliff, was a polished slab of rock with a bowl-like cavity in the center. The bowl had a diameter of one meter and a depth of 15 centimeters. A block of stone was maneuvered into the cavity by yak oxen. The block was one meter wide and one and one-half meters long. Then nineteen musical instruments were set in an arc of ninety degrees at a distance of sixty three meters from the stone slab. The radius of 63 meters was measured out accurately. The musical instruments consisted of thirteen drums and six trumpets.

"The drums were made up of eight large drums, four medium sized drums, and one small drum. The big drums and all the trumpets were fixed on mounts which would be adjusted with staffs in the direction of the slab of stone. The drums were made of 3mm thick sheet iron, and had a weight of 150 kg. They were built in five sections. All the drums were open at one end, while the other end had a bottom of metal, on which the monks beat with big leather clubs. Behind each instrument was a row of monks.

"When the stone was in position, the monk behind the small drum gave a signal to start. The small drum had a very sharp sound, and could be heard even with the other instruments making a terrible din. All the monks were singing and chanting a prayer, slowly increasing the tempo of this unbelievable noise. During the first four minutes nothing happened, then as the speed of the drumming, and the noise, increased, the big stone block started to rock and sway, and suddenly it took off into the air with an increasing speed in the direction of the platform in front of the cave hole 250 meters high. After three minutes of ascent it landed on the platform.

"Continuously, they brought new blocks to the meadow, and the monks using this method, transported five to six blocks per hour on a parabolic flight track approximately 500 meters long and 250 meters high. From time to time, a stone split, and the monks moved the split stones away."

The report concludes by noting that to prove he was not going mad, the doctor made two different films of the levitation. The society for which Dr. Jarl was working for, confiscated the movies and declared them classified. To this day, the films have not been released for public viewing.

Bruce Cathie has spent a good part of his life working with mathematics and mapping the Earth's energy grid systems. He offers a good explanation for levitation based upon his research as well as the investigations of others:

"The sound waves being generated by the combination of instruments were directed in such a way that an anti-gravitational effect was created at the center of focus (position of the stones) and around the periphery, or the arc, of a third of a circle through which the stones moved."

Cathie concludes that the Tibetans as well as the Egyptians, and possibly the original inhabitants of Atlantis "had possession of the secrets relating to the geometric structure of matter, and the methods of manipulating the harmonic values." Cathie believes that the Tibetans were able to defy the laws of gravity and actually possessed devices which could travel through the air as if they were weightless. He believes that by studying ancient records, we may soon be able to construct a type of "flying saucer" or floating disc of our own that will be the forerunner of humankind actually learning to levitate objects, as well as ourselves, on a permanent basis.

THE INCREDIBLE POWERS OF BORIS ERMOLAEV

The iron curtain has been down for a number of years. The Soviet Union no longer exists. Information that had once been forbidden has now become available to those seeking the truth. However, despite the new freedoms enjoyed by the people of Russia, some things still remain a mystery.

Take for instance the strange powers of Boris Ermolaev. At one time the Russian film director's exploits filled Soviet scientific journals. Now however, Ermolaev has faded back into obscurity, with no easy answers to his unusual powers. Soviet scientists were convinced that Ermolaev had genuine paranormal abilities. Genady Sergeyev, a doctor of engineering and a consultant mathematician was certain of Ermolaev's powers: "Ermolaev has the unusual ability of concentrating his energy into a focal point in mid-air and causing objects to be suspended in the air for many seconds."

Professor Venyamin Pushkin has worked several times with Ermolaev in carefully controlled government authorized experiments. Pushkin wrote in a scientific journal, "There are actually people who possess the capacity of influencing objects so that they remain suspended in mid-air. I have witnessed Ermolaev suspend objects in mid-air. I believe this man is capable of creating a magnetic field that defies gravity."

114

LEVITATION AND INVISIBILITY

The experiments took place in 1973 and 1974 in laboratories at Moscow University. Pushkin published an official report in which he said that each experiment was preceded by warm-up exercises so that Ermolaev could reach a state of high tension.

When this was done, Ermolaev started with simple demonstrations. He placed his hands over a spread-out deck of cards, face down, and correctly named each card's suit and value. Ermolaev then moved objects on a table without touching them. After that he attacked the major part of his experiment. Pushkin wrote: "Ermolaev took an object in his hands, pressed it between his outstretched hands, then slowly moved his hands apart. The object remained hanging in mid-air. He continued to move his hands till each palm was about eight inches clear of the object. It remained in mid-air for a number of seconds."

Another authority who witnessed Ermolaev at work was Ivan Guderman, science editor of the newspaper Evening Sverdlosk. Guderman has made numerous important contributions to psychic research. He was permitted to view some of the experiments that took place.

"The room is empty except for a table in the middle. On it, a ping-pong ball, a box of matches, and several pencils. A man walks into the room, stops in front of the table, stretches out his hand, freezes, but by the expression on his face, by the tension of his body, one knows that he just doesn't stand there, he is working.

"A minute goes by, another. Suddenly the ball is jerked from its position and is rolling off the table. The box is also moving, as though sliding across the surface of the table. The pencils seem to have lost their gravity and have risen into the air."

What is Ermolaev's magic? Pushkin's original thought was that static electricity played a part. The electrical charges made the objects move. Further experiments, however, proved that such was not the case. There was no way that static electricity could make pencils levitate. Pushkin then wrote in his report:

"I then considered the theory of one of our scientists, A.P. Dubrov. Its essence is that living systems are capable of originating and receiving gravitational waves. To accept this, one must accept the most unusual assumption that man is able to give birth to a gravitational field and then, with its help, affect surrounding objects. I was able to cross-check this theory with the strong evidence offered in the experiments with Ermolaev."

Pushkin stressed the point that it was merely theoretical that Ermolaev was able to create gravitational fields. He wrote: "The tradition of science invokes certain taboos in areas that deal with a violation of fundamental laws of nature. The ability of man to affect objects near him is still considered by numbers of scientists as something pertaining to violation of the basic laws of nature. However, what is essential and should be stressed time and time again is that feats of moving and suspending objects in the air, with all their unusual and mind-boggling aspects, do not contradict the existing framework of physics.

Ermolaev has also levitated people. One was a famous Russian actress who preferred not to have her name mentioned. With a small audience watching, Ermolaev lifted her about four feet into the air while she was in a prone position. He managed to keep her suspended for about 20 seconds.

No one to date has quite explained to any satisfaction how Boris Ermolaev was able to create levitation. What is known is that when he levitated anything, either an object or a person, he suffered extreme trauma. His body would tremble, he would sweat, his heart rate would increase, his concentration reached a depth that most of us can never attain. He was totally immersed in what he was doing.

Those who have mastered the phenomenon, like Boris Ermolaev, say it is much easier to levitate objects that are light in weight. The suggestion is that you try it with pencils, paper clips and rubber bands. Move those objects before you try to levitate yourself

Concentration is the key. Have absolutely no distractions. Do it alone so that you won't feel self-conscious. Once your thoughts start to wander, take a break. Concentrate in short periods of time until you can increase the span.

When you have mastered the light objects, try levitating a bridge table. Remember, table tipping is not levitation. The table must rise straight up, with all four legs off the floor. It helps if you are psychic. Most likely you know that you are, but are not sure to what extent. There are no measurements. Levitation may let you know just how psychic you really are.

Perhaps Ermolaev had discovered the secrets of the Siddha's. The ancient wisdom that only the dedicated could ever dream of mastering. To know such secrets would take years of spiritual quests and mental mastery. Or maybe Ermolaev was born with the natural ability of levitation already in place, ready to go at the slightest need. Maybe the Saints and other Holy men who levitated during religious ecstasy were also such "naturals." These natural powers could also act as a beacon to those who have the ability to "see" such energy in humans.

In ***The Metal Benders***, John Hasted reports that: "In 1977 a young Soviet physicist, August Stern, defected to the West and related some of his experiences in parapsychology. He had worked in the Siberian science city of Novosibirsk" with about fifty scientists who induced levitation by enclosing a subject "within a cube of mirrors. The multiple images, apparently stretching in all directions to infinity, have the effect of disorienting the subject, who then levitates if he has the ability."

Hasted tried the same experiment but was unsuccessful. He speculated that levitation could perhaps be seen as "a continual rapid series of teleportation events, each to a position very slightly removed from its predecessor; this would produce the appearance of continuous movement or suspension.

There are a few reports that some people who have been seen levitating were also surrounded by a brilliant light, sometimes in the form of a beam and sometimes as a general illumination. For example, in 1608 the mystic St Bernardino Realino was seen to be levitating nearly a meter off the ground in the kneeling position while praying in his room at his monastery in Lecce, in southern Italy. The saint was radiating light so brightly that the witness, Tobias de Ponte, had initially thought that the room was on fire in. It is unclear whether this radiance is connected to human levitation or whether these are different paranormal phenomena that sometimes occur together.

URI GELLER'S MYSTERIOUS POWERS OF LEVITATION

The notion that the mind, or consciousness, can manipulate matter through time and space has been demonstrated throughout history in poltergeist occurrences. A poltergeist is thought to be either the unconscious psychokinetic energy of a living individual, or a traditional haunting. Either way, an as yet unknown aspect of consciousness controls the manipulation of matter.

A poltergeist is considered to be an uncontrolled outburst of psychokinesis exhibiting an almost rudimentary intelligence. But what about controlled psychokinesis; someone who is deliberately trying to use mind powers to manipulate matter? Is there any evidence that you can literally use the force of your "will" to move things around, levitate, or even make them disappear?

One such person, who claims that he has the power to influence objects with his mind, and has the evidence to back up his claims, is Uri Geller. Uri Geller was born in Israel on December 20, 1946. His parents are of Hungarian and Austrian descent and he is distantly related on his mother's side to Sigmund Freud. At the age of four he had a mysterious encounter with a sphere of light while in a garden near his house. He has often wondered if this strange encounter was somehow responsible for his unusual abilities.

Geller first became aware of his powers when he was five. One day, during a meal, his spoon curled up in his hand and broke, although he had applied no physical pressure to it. His parents were shocked and Uri did not mention the incident to anyone else at that time. Later, he developed these powers in school with demonstrations to fellow pupils. His mother thought he had inherited them from Sigmund Freud.

When he was eleven, he went to live in Cyprus, where he remained until he was seventeen. He then returned to Israel, served as a paratrooper in the Israel army and fought in the Six Day War of 1967 during which he was wounded in action. From 1968 to 1969 Uri worked as a model, he was photographed for many different advertisements.

In 1969 he began to demonstrate his powers of telepathy and psychokinesis to small audiences. By the end of 1971, however, his was a household name throughout Israel thanks to his numerous stage appearances. He was given a plug by then Prime Minister, Golda Meir. When asked on a national radio program what she predicted for the future of Israel, she replied, "Don't ask me - ask Uri Geller!"

In 1972, Uri left Israel for Europe, where he attracted widespread attention. In Germany, witnessed by reporters and photographers, he stopped a cable car in mid air using only the power of his mind. He then did the same to an escalator in a major department store. That same year he traveled to the United States at the invitation of Apollo 14 astronaut Captain Edgar Mitchell, as well as inventor and author Andrija Puharich MD. Among the notable scientists he met were Professor Gerald Feinberg of Columbia University's physics Department, Ronald Hawke from the Lawrence Livermore National Laboratory, Ron Robertson of the Atomic Energy Commission and NASA's Dr Wernher von Braun, "Father of the Space Age," who testified that his own wedding ring bent in his hand without being touched at any time by Geller.

Geller toured the United States giving lectures and demonstrations, but comparatively few scientists were convinced that his powers were real and not the result of chicanery. He also performed on American television that resulted in hundreds of telephone calls from all across the country from families who reported cutlery bending in their home as they watched him on their TV sets.

In Britain Geller made several successful public television records of apparently paranormal bending of cutlery, and many children came forward and claimed, sometimes even demonstrated, similar happenings. Mathematical physicist John Taylor, who was present in the studio, started a program of fieldwork and invited numbers of the children to his laboratory. He published accounts in a book entitled Superminds and publicly affirmed that he believed paranormal metal bending was a real effect.

As of the writing of this book, no one has yet to prove beyond a shadow of a doubt that Uri Geller's amazing abilities are not real. In fact, Geller has proved himself, at least in a financial way, by using his powers as a paid consultant to locate oil and valuable minerals. His success in this field has made him a very wealthy man, all of this from the humble origins of a spoon-bender.

THE POLTERGEIST CONNECTION

The poltergeist phenomena has been extensively researched and studied over the years. Psychic researchers have sifted through firsthand accounts, judging them by the same criteria as those applied to historical, anthropological and forensic source material. Other psychic researchers have been fortunate enough to witness for themselves poltergeist phenomena, and have written some fascinating accounts as a result.

On this basis most scholars have concluded that strange, physical phenomena really do occur on a somewhat regular basis. The modern technical term for physical poltergeist phenomena is RSPK (recurrent spontaneous psychokinesis).

In a poltergeist case, objects have been observed to spontaneously fly about the house, apparently in a random way. Sometimes their paths of flight are unnaturally crooked, and often the objects are not seen to leave their normal positions; sometimes they just appear in the air, in full view of witnesses, and gently drop to the floor.

Some objects, when picked up immediately after their levitation are found to be warm. Sometimes they arrive with spin, or angular momentum. Other times they appear in motion, their flight starting from a position different from their normal place. Sometimes the origin of the objects is unknown, as in the cases where showers of stones are reported.

Furniture can move spontaneously about the room, tip over, and even levitate and crash down again on the floor. Sometimes these movements are observed; sometimes they happen when no one is in the room.

A typical poltergeist case will last only for a period of weeks or months. The spontaneity of the movements has led to the opinion that the phenomena are caused by a ghost. However, the more usually accepted view is that one or more of the personalities involved, usually children; are unconsciously responsible for the phenomena, in that they are physically present when they occur.

Such personalities have been called epicenters (although this term is also used to describe the area of the house in which events most frequently happen). When the subject realizes that he or she is 'responsible,' and is now the center of attention, they will often add to the effects by normal physical means. Extraordinary and strange events, including many quasi physical as opposed to physical phenomena, have been reported in poltergeist cases, but the above are the most usual and the most relevant to psychokinesis, invisibility and levitation.

John B. Hasted in his book **The Metal-Benders** (1981, Routledge & Kegan Paul) makes the observation that the particular type of poltergeist event he has observed most frequently is the traveling of an object from one location to another in an abnormal way. It might best be described as the disappearance of the object in its original position, and its reappearance somewhere else. In other words - teleportation; which is closely related to invisibility, levitation and is of physical similarity and relevance to metal bending.

In November 1974, Hasted and his wife, Lynn, were paid a visit one Saturday afternoon by Uri Geller and two friends. Hasted had already met Uri on several occasions and had observed his metal bending. But Lynn had never spoken to Uri and had never seen anything bend. She was strongly skeptical, and had never had the slightest interest in psychic phenomena.

Lynn served drinks in the lounge, and the guests commented on the carvings displayed on the piano and bookshelves. Lynn took Uri into the kitchen to get him an apple while the others stayed in the lounge. Lynn had started to tell Geller that she was entirely skeptical about metal bending.

John Hasted was just entering the kitchen when he clearly saw a small object appear a few feet in the air and fall to the floor in front of the back door. Geller turned round to face it, and they saw that it was a small Japanese marine ivory statuette of an old peasant. This had been in its normal place on the bookshelf in the lounge. They were certain that the statuette had not been thrown, as it would have described a trajectory instead of dropping more or less straight downward. If Geller had thrown the statuette it would have bounced into the corner instead of dropping downwards. Moreover Geller had his back to its landing place, and his hands were in front of him, with an apple in one.

While everyone was standing around looking at the statuette, a second object appeared in the air and dropped. This time everyone observed it, and it was clear that it had not been thrown. This object was the key of a Buhl clock that stands next to the statuette on the bookshelf in the lounge.

Hasted comments that if the statuette and the key had passed in normal parabolic arcs from the lounge bookcase straight to their destination in the kitchen, then the objects would have had to pass through a wall to get to the place at which they reappeared. After Gellers visit, Hasted recorded over forty psychokinetic episodes in his house.

LEVITATION AND INVISIBILITY

One incident occurred on December 23, 1974 as the family was preparing a turkey for Christmas dinner. The turkey was wrapped in a plastic bag and was resting on a tray on the bare white plastic table top. Beside the turkey, on the tray and wrapped in another plastic bag fastened with wires, were the giblets, liver, etc. Suddenly a brown object appeared on the table in front of us, and I thought for a moment that it might be a leaf that had floated in through a window. But it was in fact a turkey liver, and we checked that one was no longer in the sealed plastic bag with the giblets. It resembled the other turkey liver, which we found to be safely in its own bag in the larder.

There was no smear of blood on the white table, such as the liver would have made if it had moved along the surface. There had been no sound, and there seemed to us no normal explanation. I did check with our butcher that it was actually a turkey liver.

This event was one of the most significant I had observed, since the liver in all reasonable certainty started from its situation inside the sealed plastic bag, and finished outside it. All three of us saw first of all an expanse of white table, and immediately afterwards a piece of liver on it. There were no holes in the plastic bag, although it was not vacuum tight.

John Hasted continued to have levitation and teleportation experiences in the presence of Uri Geller. During July 1975 Hasted was exposed to a short but rapid sequence of teleportation's while staying in the New Otani Hotel, Tokyo, in the room next to Uri Geller. About 10:30 PM one evening after a press conference during which there had been a miscalculation that upset Geller, his secretary Trina and photographer Shipi departed to send a Telex message. Hasted left Geller in his room, and unlocked the door to his room and went in. Within a few seconds he saw a small object fall to the floor, not from a great height, but within one foot of the drawn window curtains. It was a pair of nail clippers.

When he took the clippers next door to Uri, he told Hasted that it belonged to him, and would normally be kept zipped up in a leather case from which he showed that it was missing. While they were speaking, a glass tumbler dropped to the carpet behind them, in the center of the room.

Hasted took Geller back to his room to show him where the nail clippers had fallen, but they got no further than opening the door when there was an explosion and crash. Broken glass was found all over the area by the door, and in the hotel corridor. One glass tumbler from the bathroom was now missing. Hotel guests in the corridor saw the flying glass but could offer no explanation.

Uri returned to his room and Hasted almost immediately saw the sudden appearance of his magnifying glass in the middle of the floor. By good luck it was reasonably well in his field of vision at the time, so that he was able to be certain that it did not just fall to the ground. Previously it had been on the desk, more than six feet away.

Based on his own observations, Hasted summarized some important features of the teleportation phenomenon. For obvious reasons, it is much more usual for the appearance than for the disappearance to be observed. Indeed, it would be very difficult to be certain that both things happen at exactly the same moment (say within 0.2 sec) without some instrumentation. On rare occasions the disappearance and reappearance locations are both within the field of vision. Which begs the question, did these objects become invisible before they were levitated, or teleported?

The reappearance can take place either in the air or on a surface such as floor or table. Accounts exist of objects reappearing inside solids, particularly fruit. Teleportation's into identified hens' eggs have also been reported.

Reappearing objects have often been observed to appear with their own angular momentum. I have seen objects spin rapidly as they fall to, or appear on, the floor. It is difficult to make generalizations about direction of rotation or orientation of the axis of spin.

In many poltergeist-induced levitations, linear momentum is reported to be associated with an object at the moment of its reappearance. Detailed accounts by Maurice Gross, the Society for Psychical Research investigator of the Enfield poltergeist, mentions glass marbles that flew about the room; there was no question that these marbles were simply teleporting, and did not have flight trajectories; they could be seen in flight; but the problem of where their trajectories started was more difficult.

They seemed to start from the closed window, yet there were no marbles on the windowsill. The most likely alternative was that they had teleported to the window and appeared with linear momentum into the room. This feature might offer a clue to the 'dog leg' flight paths that are sometimes observed in poltergeist cases, and were seen at Enfield. In these paths there is a sudden change of direction in mid flight. This might be interpreted as a teleportation in mid flight, to a position almost identical with the point of invisibility, but with the appearance associated with a new linear momentum vector.

Sometimes the object after its reappearance is felt to be warmer than normal. Reports of the appearance of warm objects have appeared fairly frequently in the literature of poltergeist phenomena.

On rare occasions the disappearance of an object is observed several minutes or even hours before its reappearance. A disappearance is noticed, and at a later time the reappearance of the object is also observed. There is no question that the object was at the location of the reappearance for all of the interim period; this location remained exposed to the field of view of observers, and was usually an obvious one.

Very little has been observed which supports the hypothesis of gradual rather than sudden appearance. The gradual appearance and gradual disappearance of apparitions would seem to be a different phenomenon, at least as regards the long times of appearance. At the Stanford Research Institute, during Uri Geller's visit, an interesting video tape was made of a wristwatch falling through the field of view onto a table.

Although it seems that the appearance took place above the field of view, the watch is seen to flicker as it descends; in consecutive frames the light reflected from the watch increases and decreases. One might be tempted to regard this as an 'oscillation in the intensity of the appearance,' but a more likely interpretation is that the presence of angular momentum causes the light reflected from the watch to vary periodically. A very interesting claim has been made by Dr Miyauchi that Masuaki Kiyota has materialized (or teleported) a full Coca Cola bottle in stages; the bottom first, and then the top.

Information is slowly accumulating about teleportation's of living creatures, including human beings. Hasted relates that he has never witnessed such events himself, but has received reports from various victims and from their families. Very little information is available about larger creatures, but Hasted once received a detailed report from Matthew Thompson, a poultry farmer in Dorset, which he summarized as follows: " I have within recent weeks had two separate instances of birds (caged chickens) disappearing and reappearing some hours later. I am talking about birds disappearing literally into thin air and being neither visible nor audible. Any possibility of them being removed by some other persons and then returned can be completely ruled out."

Andrija Puharich, who also spent much time studying Uri Geller recalled the time when Uri found himself unexpectedly teleported to Puharich's home. Geller was with a woman named Maria Janis (Gary Cooper's daughter). He left the apartment they were in to go jogging. Within two minutes of leaving 68th and Park in New York, he somehow landed in Ossining which is 36 miles away. I was home alone. I heard this huge crash and thought it was an earthquake. I couldn't find the source of it at first, and then I heard this bleak voice, "Andrija! Andrija!" There he was crumpled up on the floor. He was intact and wasn't hurt, but the shock he experienced was considerable, and the event was never repeated. I've had a lot of that kind of stuff with Uri.

Geller remembers the incident very clearly: "I was jogging in Manhattan when the next thing I remembered was that I was thrown at something and I crashed through something on to a table then fell on the floor And I looked around and I was... you'll find it unbelievable, but I was in Ossining, a small town 36 miles out of Manhattan in the porch of Andrija Puharich.

I shouted his name 'Andrija! Andrija!' and it took him five minutes to find me. He went out of the house to look for footprints in the snow, but of course there were none."

One of the most unusual claims made by Puharich regarding the talents of Uri Geller involves Geller's alleged ability to teleport automobiles. Since Puharich's book, several other reports on auto teleportation have been filed.

Ray Stanford of Austin, Texas reported that after he used his car to pick up Geller at the airport, his automobile was apparently teleported. One of these involved an automobile accident. Testimony from witnesses is recorded in the traffic court transcripts. They observed Stanford's car suddenly appear in front of them, "like a light that had been switched on." The distance of this teleportation was about fifty feet.

On the second occasion, the teleportation was even more dramatic. Driving with his wife along Interstate 10 in Texas, Ray suddenly noticed a silvery metallic, blue glow around the car. Stuck in heavy traffic at the time, he actually mentioned to his wife he hoped "Uri's intelligences would teleport us away from here."

Then, according to his testimony he felt a strange sensation in his brain and the scene instantly changed. They had traveled thirty seven miles in no time and using no gas. Later, as the car was not functioning well, it was hauled to a garage. The alternator and voltage regulator were completely burned out and all the wiring was completely charred.

One family of a young metal-bender told John Hasted that they would continually find their son in unnatural places, wedged in between wardrobe top and ceiling, and so on. They would be running a hot bath for him, and suddenly a scream would announce his "transportation" from his bedroom into the overheated bath, for which he was totally unprepared. The affliction of this family lasted for several months, but eventually grew less serious.

One test subject named Nicholas Williams also claims to have been teleported out of a locked room. When his father pointed out that this left them with a problem of the key remaining on the inside, Nicholas teleported back again to unlock the door. He has described the experience as something like being in a blizzard.

Due to the extensive research done with Uri Geller and others like him, scientific communities in China, the United States and other countries are now identifying small groups of infants and children that display rare abilities such as purging HIV, advanced genius and psychic/telekinetic abilities and other extra ordinary attributes.

LEVITATION AND INVISIBILITY

Usually the phenomena are first noticed after a television appearance by Uri Geller. When the household first becomes aware of the bendings, it is often not known who is responsible. Nearly always it is one of the children, who finds that if he or she strokes a spoon between fingers and thumb it sometimes softens and bends.

These children can display some or all of these qualities and others not yet identified. In these children, fragments of DNA science identifies as 'junk DNA' and other portions of the DNA chain that science has yet to identify, are more organized and operational at birth than in the average populations, which gives these special children biological, mental and/or spiritual skills and abilities that appear advanced, compared to that of the norm.

One little understood attribute of Indigo advancement is that of perceptual expansion, an accelerated psycho spiritual biological orientation and natural usage of sensory abilities that are beyond the range of the commonly known five senses. The phenomena of perceptual expansion due to genetic progress is presently evidenced and demonstrated in global culture through rapidly increasing occurrences and reports of unexplained events such as ESP, near death experiences, out of body experiences, angelic encounters, hauntings, interdimensional communications, teleportation, UFO abduction, lucid dreaming, invisibility and levitation.

Exactly how these superminds are producing psychokinetic energy to bend metal, levitate, or teleport objects is not fully understood, but there seem to be two or three possible mechanisms, some combination of which may act at a given time.

- First there is evidence that a physical force may act on the metal and that this may be independent of the size of the region that it acts on.

- Second, groups of atoms may stop interacting with others and so be able to pass through from one location to another. This is the same phenomenon where objects pass through walls in poltergeist cases. An object may either be invisible as during teleportation or it can start to return, be visible, but not feel gravitational forces fully and gently float to the ground.

- Finally it returns to the real world. Beeping calculators have been teleported and the sound could be heard coming first from one location and then another, until it is at last returned. Small radio transmitters have also been teleported by Chinese children. The possibility that there may be an as yet poorly understood interaction between particles and space-time is discussed in theoretical physics textbooks.

LEVITATION AND INVISIBILITY

It is acknowledged that curved space-time can create particles. The reverse may occur under some as yet unknown conditions. What has not yet been investigated (as the full theory of quantum gravity is unknown) is the possible duality between systems of particles (and the information they contain) and gravitational waves / space-time curvature.

Systems may be of greater interest because of the additional information that they contain second quantization and so on. Quantum coherence allows pairs of particles to easily penetrate a barrier in a Josephson junction with an enhanced probability and a similar effect occurs in the laser where the barrier to photon decay is lowered by the coherent radiation stream. Physicists are just starting to apply these ideas to coherent matter waves. The final mechanism behind paranormal phenomena seems more common throughout recorded history than in the laboratory and involves more fundamental changes in reality such as substitution of parts of an object for another one or temporary duplication. It seems that some minds under some conditions can cause temporary construction of an object (such as a deceased person or duplication of their own body) partial dematerialization may also accompany this.

This could be a similar mechanism to the reality shifts observed when a psychic converts one object into another. It points to an abstract representation of objects in the world of physics and the mind being able to tap into this. This would also explain the claims of many psychics that they are not doing anything and that there must be some other external 'intelligence' involved.

There may be a natural hierarchy of abstract levels of representation in nature. Interestingly developing some of these skills seems to be on a fairly well mapped out path among meditators and Yoga masters. Such systems, if they exist, might be expected to behave more in accordance to our bureaucratic structures.

Uri Geller has his own opinion on the mysterious nature of invisibility and levitation: "I think it is some kind of automatic process with us, it's the sharpening of our inner powers, our mind, our brain, our spirit, our soul. I don't think we are going to build some kind of time machine. I think our minds will be able to move us about. But I'm not talking around the corner; I'm talking 250,000 years from now."

TELEKINESIS – THE KEY TO LEVITATION

Telekinesis (TK): Is it a scientific phenomenon, or is it paranormal? Scientific community will tell us that magic can't happen, yet there are innumerable supposed cases of supernatural activities throughout history. To bridge a barrier between science and occult, we can say that telekinetic ability is not necessarily witchcraft or sorcery. It's sheer mind power. Telekinesis can happen, all you have to do is put your mind over matter.

Telekinesis is the ability to move things using the power of mind. This is done without using any physical devices. At first, this may seem unreal, but as your powers grow you'll learn to appreciate it. As every mass or matter is made up of molecules, an experienced person will tell you that it's just a matter of communicating with these molecules. Once you are adept at doing so, you will be able to move things using your own telekinetic abilities. This is the first step to being able to actually levitate yourself. A piece of advice though, telekinesis is something which cannot be achieved overnight. Some people require less amount of time while some may require more time to master this technique. So, patience is the key to this art. Listed below are a few exercises for a beginner in telekinesis. Using lighter objects will give you faster results.

Since you wish to move or distort things through the power of your thoughts, it only makes sense to start with improving your concentration. There is no such thing as a genie in a bottle, in which case you simply make a wish and it comes true. You have to work towards it. Meditating and improving your concentration will keep unwanted thoughts away.

Put up a soothing picture on a wall and start focusing on that picture. Make sure that there are no other wall hangings or distractions around there. Concentrate in such a way that no divergent thoughts come to your mind. Your attention should be centered only on the picture. This may be difficult in the beginning, but in time, you will learn to push other thoughts away. For starters, you can even use a dot instead of a picture. In later stages, you must learn to hold your concentration for longer periods and also be able to merge yourself with the image you view.

The energy of the mind is called PSI energy in psychokinetical terms. It is one of the basic elements of psychokinesis. You detect auras and classify them as good and bad depending on the energies they emit. You can try doing this with food products as though you were using them for the first time by deleting all your memories associated with them temporarily; and then finding out whether the aura appears negative or positive to you.

Pretend that you are the only thing that exists in this universe. Imagine that everything else including your surroundings, sounds, smells are absent. The instant realization of the energy inside of you gives you a tingle. This is nothing but a manifestation of the potential that can be good or bad for you depending on the state of your mind. Give yourself some time and you will be able to sense energies present in all other beings and objects too. It is the force fundamental that actually initializes your telekinetic powers. You need to have an emotion and intensify it and finally channelize yourself via the mind's eye.

Take a smooth pen and place it on a table where there is no perturbation. Try moving it just by thought. Once it moves, try stopping it the same way.

Projecting yourself from an astral or emotional plane to a mental plane is what comprises a mental projection. Similarly, leaving the physical body to send your inner self off to an astral plane is an astral projection.

For first time experiences, look for places you are familiar with. Make yourself comfortable and do some breathing exercises before you start visualizing the plane you want to project yourself to. Close your eyes to inhibit the surroundings and go into the dream state. Once you get back validate the reality by moving your hand or performing some other pre-decided action. It is not recommended to this exercise for longer than 15 minutes for beginners to prevent yourself from losing control.

You need to try telekinesis for quite some time before coming to the realization of it. Popular exercises will keep your enthusiasm intact till you finally achieve success. Please don't be disheartened if this doesn't happen right away. The possibility of it happening straightaway is very little. Success will follow after many trials and errors. And when you do experience some telekinetic activity, there's no telling whether you might be able to demonstrate it to others again the very next moment. Maintain a journal of what you have achieved. Mind you, this journal is only for yourself to check the progress you have made.

Bending a Spoon: Remember that scene in the movie "Matrix", where Neo is visiting Oracle for the first time? He sees a kid who was able to bend a spoon in many directions. Well, telekinesis is something similar to that (although the kid was playing with the proverbial Matrix and not actually performing telekinesis). As I have mentioned before, a beginner should always choose lighter objects, preferably a paper or a pen. Assuming that you have enough concentrating power, concentrate all your thoughts on an object that you choose. Let us assume that you've chosen a paper.

Close your eyes, focus your mind and start visualizing the movement of the paper. With clarity of thought, focus on paper and visualize yourself communicating with that object. Concentrate your senses of sight, sound, colors, etc., to communicate with that piece of paper. Do this only for ten to fifteen minutes. Do not overstretch yourself.

The PSI Ball: Simply rub your hands for a few minutes and place them apart. You will feel some sort of magnetism between them. Intensify it till you see a ball made of color bands. This might take years to accomplish. When you do, feel the energy between your hand and the ball. You can even create protective energy shields out of these balls. In advanced stages, you can learn to take decisions for them and pass them on. PSI Wheels can also be used for similar experiments.

The Pendulum: Use a pendulum and try to swing it without touching it. It requires your mind to become one with the pendulum. So, you must find a pendulum that is right for you. When you learn how to hold and use it properly you should be able to find lost things and search for answers. Remember, it's all in the mind.

Once you initiate your training, you need to find a proper way of advancement. This can be done in the following ways.

By hand: Manual practice is also called 'the Force'. You can do this in the first few days when you're not equipped.

Using wands or props: Any concrete objects that make you confident can be used when performing the exercises.

Verbal Incantations: Chants also boost morale and can be very useful in making people aware of their internal energies.

Using imagination: Imagining magnetic or invisible objects/hands or some sort of stringed connection during execution can get you closer to your goals. You can also imagine a fictional character doing it for you. Better still, you can pretend to be a being of superpower yourself.

Inception of an idea in the mind can lead to telekinetic abilities in dreams. Running, morphing, diving, flying, traveling through portals, swapping perspectives, etc., can be great ideas for such dreams. Although, it is not proven that they help telekinesis in real life, they can actually give a feel of the same to a beginner.

A FEW EXERCISES

You can enhance your brain power by the following activities. Remember not to dislocate objects by hand or your breath while experimenting.

Rolling the edges of a plain paper.
Floating a toothpick in a bowl.
Swinging a cork hung by a string.
Moving a compass needle clockwise or anti-clockwise. (You may use other objects, but compass needle is better as it offers very little resistance.)

LEVITATION AND INVISIBILITY

You can improve your skills through the following; You can try to get into some online courses available on the subject. But, generally they require you to adhere to their training policies and non-disclosure agreements. So, be prepared for the same.

Advanced users try to find out meaning of gemstones and extract the trapped energy of various crystals. Isochronic tones can be used to enhance powers. They can even be mixed and made by learners themselves.

There are tests to check your inborn psychic ability. They can detect how successful you can be in telekinesis. Guessing random numbers, alphabets, names, etc., can be practiced with a bunch of people. If you're alone, you can try guessing what's on a card picked from a deck.

You can flip a coin many times and try to manipulate each outcome so that the statistical average of a lot of such events (or 'individual coin flips') is deviant from the expected 50% for the unbiased coin.

Tests for tarot reading, remote viewing, etc., can also be taken. The important thing is to be honest to yourself because, in the end, we are the best to judge ourselves. Try to stick to one method per day. If using more number of methods, make sure they only differ slightly. Maximize the number of attempts for faster results.

Always keep a distance from the object you are working with so that you would not be tempted to move it by physical means. Muscles of the brain require a lot of exercise. So, keep practicing to activate your chakras and awaken extra senses. Perseverance is the key to unlock them.

Telekinesis, or any other mind exercise for that matter, requires a serene environment and peace of mind. So, always make sure you are free from external and internal disturbances. Breathing exercises and relaxing techniques always come in handy to achieve quietude.

Everyone's psychic ability differs. So, do not get disappointed if others perform quicker. Take your own time to master the skill.

Control is very crucial to any mental exercise. Learn to control yourself and use all precautionary measures where you know you could let yourself go.

For any phenomenon to receive scientific accreditation, it should be satisfactorily observable. Telekinesis results have not been satisfactory for scientists so far the results are subjective to your degree of skepticism until you experience it for yourself. Therefore, telekinesis is generally considered as paranormal activity.

CHAPTER ELEVEN
EXPOSED: LEVITATION AND THE
ANCIENT MASTERS OF WISDOM

Diane Tessman has certainly led an interesting life. She spent 11 years of her life as a school teacher. She has lived in the Virgin Islands, Florida and now resides in St. Ansgar, Iowa where she devotes much of her time to New Age activities.

Diane has her own New Age Church and channels a future human known to her as Tibus. Diane is of the opinion that Tibus channels only through her, although she has channeled other beings including, extraterrestrials, devas, angels, and Goddesses.

According to Diane, 1980 was an active one for her psychically. There were all sorts of space contacts which made themselves known to her in creative ways. For instance, in the spring of that year - May 9th to be exact -her smoke alarm started to buzz off and on. The batteries were fresh and she was not cooking at the time. The off-and-on buzzing sounded much like Morse code. Unfortunately, Diane did not know how to read the code. She did, however, take note of the time. It was 7:35 AM.

Later, when she turned on her radio, she learned that a large ship had rammed the Skyway Bridge, which stretches over Tampa Bay near St. Petersburg, Florida. Cars and buses plunged 100 feet down into the waters, killing 33 people. The time of the accident? 7:35 AM. Diane said that she feels that because she was living close to the disaster at the time, that the souls which had been torn so suddenly from their bodies had provided the energy that was manifested in the bussing of the smoke alarm.

Incidents like this one piled up during the spring and summer of 1980 and apparently prepared her for an experience she will never forget as long as she lives. Diane related her experience this way: "One night soon after I had gone to bed (I was not dreaming), I levitated through the wall: My mind was not on my space contacts and I was not meditating. I was casually churning over the worldly events of the day which had been very 'humdrum' and typical. I was lying on my stomach, as is my habit, when I abruptly felt my body rise up several feet above the bed! There was a choppy, rippling sensation much like one feels riding on an air mattress in slightly rough waters at the beach.

131

LEVITATION AND INVISIBILITY

Usually, I am not frightened when paranormal events occur or when I spot a UFO or receive a telepathic message; in fact, I long for these phenomena to occur."

Placed under hypnosis by Dr. Leo Sprinkle of the University of Wyoming, Diane Tessman recalled being abducted on board a craft from outer space at the age of six or seven. Later in life she was to experience an ongoing choir of unexplainable events including being levitated and partially pulled through a solid wall. Diane said that the sudden levitation did scare her and that she wasn't sure why until she realized that she was frightened because she was floating free through space. Now, something else had control. Upon reflection, Diane said: "Perhaps I needed a lesson in humility and trust."

Still, her experience was far from over. "I was just attempting to logically figure out my predicament without too much panic and terror, when my entire body made an abrupt right angle turn, feet first. With my last shred of calm rationale, I realized that my feet now had to be outside the wall! My single bed sat flush against an outside wall of the house. There was no room for my body to be turned sideways and still be totally within my house!"

Was it an astral journey? Diane thinks not. She has had many of them and they were never like this. She does believe that she was levitated and taken somewhere, but she has no memory of the trip. She remembers rising up from the bed and then being outside the wall and trying desperately to get back inside.

Says Diane: "I had great difficulty in getting my eyes open. It was a very strange feeling because it seemed that I had two sets of eyes; I could open one set with great effort but they would not function, could not see the reality I had come from but only a calm, black, other-dimensional place. Finally, after several minutes of attempting to fight panic and asserting my own will with all my strength, my 'other' set of eyes opened and I was back in bed."

Again, Diane thinks the adventure may have been brought about to teach her humility, trust and faith. In any event, she had a similar experience several weeks later, and had the same terrified reaction. "This time," says Diane, "I was lying on my back, eyes open and totally awake. Just as before. Without warning my bed began to dump me out the wall! I remember realizing that I was totally outside the wall...and then I have no recollection of events until I desperately struggled to return to my bed."

There was a bizarre piece of physical evidence accompanying both weird abductions. The battery of her car parked outside the house was drained on both occasions. In many UFO encounters, car batteries and their casings are damaged or ruined because of the strong electromagnetic fields around UFOs. These fields usually destroy batteries and car ignition systems.

LEVITATION AND INVISIBILITY

On the surface it appeared that Diane Tessman levitated and perhaps also became invisible. Slipping through the wall tells us that there must have been some sort of invisibility involved (either of her or the wall). Up till this point in her life, this remarkable woman had touched on all phases of the paranormal except levitation and invisibility. Could it be that her other-dimensional contacts now wanted her to become proficient in these arts as well?

What we do know about Diane Tessman is that the longer you are in her company the more certain you are that she is a woman who has touched the unknown. She has also come in physical contact with other-world aliens — and has the scar to prove it.

Diane has a scar that runs between her nose and lip. It is extremely straight. The scar is so deep that the tissue goes all the way through to the inside of her mouth.

Diane has had it nearly all of her life. She doesn't know how she got it. She has investigated every possibility. Her mother insists that Diane never cut herself there as a child and never has had even minor corrective surgery. Diane has checked with the hospital, but there is no record of any extra expense for facial surgery. The scar itself looks exactly like it was done by a surgeon's scalpel, yet no one in her family can remember such an operation.

Diane also noted that the scar is in the exact spot in which a surgeon would cut if he wanted to enter the brain with a scalpel or a laser beam. The procedure eliminates the barrier that the skull represents. Was her scar placed there by UFO beings during one of her abductions? Diane Tessman can't be sure, although she does feel that she has had psychic surgery of some kind, and with a purpose that is beyond her.

"While many of those in contact with Higher Realms do not have unknown scars, others of us do," Diane points out. "The Star Children are the ones who have the majority of scars, due to surgery in early childhood or blood or tissue samples taken in early childhood abductions. It is neither an honor nor a disgrace to have a scar due to your contact with UFO beings or with Higher Realms. We all have diverse and unique purposes on our survival path through the turmoil of the End Days. All of us are equal and all of us are One."

Are there any good explanations to account for the strange powers of invisibility and levitation? It is conceivable that there isn't any one process by which these abilities take place. Any breakthrough in our understanding of these powers will come only when the scientific community can observe and study human invisibility and levitation in controlled conditions.

Unfortunately, there are few contemporary psychics who seem capable of reproducing these feats in the laboratory. Perhaps our only alternative lies in the mystic East, with some yogic master who would be willing to demonstrate his abilities under careful scientific scrutiny. If it is pursued, it may only be a short time before mankind is able to learn levitation as easily as you could learn the technique of hypnotism. Then, and only then will these amazing powers be understood and developed, hopefully for the betterment of all mankind.

CHAPTER TWELVE
THE WEIRD SCIENCE BEHIND INVISIBILITY AND LEVITATION

Mysterious disappearances have confounded and entranced people for thousands of years, from Enoch's sudden disappearance to Ambrose Bierce's popular 1880's articles of people disappearing while simply walking in a field. But one thing is consistent within the stories, whether true or false, a vortex or funnel is often written in. For Bierce, these were invisible funnels within a prairie, or anywhere, into which an unsuspecting person walked and was held in a different time or space, though certainly Space-Time Warps were not even a part of scientific or popular vernacular in the 1880s. For Elijah, he was taken away in a "fiery whirlwind," a vortex. For Ezekiel's vision, vortexes turned within whirlwinds.

For the cynical these were only fanciful stories, and Bierce's were Saturday afternoon mystery magazine pulp. But literature has an uncanny way of being prophetic. In the great scientific age of the 20th century, it was discovered that all matter is actually at a level of vortex kinesis, that is, swirling or spiraling motion. Whether it is the great galaxies, planets, suns, or the smallest atoms, all things rotate upon an axis and revolve around a core. The natural action of energy is vortex kinesis.

With the 20th century there came mankind's ability to support a thriving scientific culture. This allowed men of science to start contemplating such things as space-time warps. Perhaps they were urged to do so because of popular belief in such topics as expressed in Bierce's Saturday afternoon pulp or in such popular occult stories as Oliver Lerch's sudden vanishing.

The truth or falsehood of these stories is not important here. What is important is that they captured popular imagination, and perhaps made it acceptable for men of science to speak in serious terms about their possibility.

The most famous to give rational body to the idea of space-time warps was undoubtedly Dr. Albert Einstein. His own quote, one of my favorites, set the tenor for his modis operandi for scientific discovery: "Science is merely the refinement of everyday thinking."

Using his "Thought Experiments," his scientific knowledge allowed him to temper and direct his imagination. Thus while other physicists came out of school with the same education he had, they went on to perform only the mechanics of physics, but not the artistry that Einstein would pioneer. In essence, he sat back and thought; he considered; he imagined. These were not flights of fancy; they were based on facts established and rational inference from observed data.

He imagined himself speeding in space, and came up with Relativity. He postulated that gravity was not a force at all, but a curvature of space around a massive body, like a planet, speeding through space. He further postulated that time was continuous with space.

An example may help us to understand. Two speeding cars pacing each other seem not to be moving at all to those inside each. But to a person standing on the side of the road, the cars zoom past at fantastic speed and are gone. But to those inside, life would remain the same; they would see the next car pacing them. It would be the same because they are being propelled at the same speed as the cars. Our planet is like one of those cars: it is being propelled in space, and us along with it.

The car can be considered in a progression of time as well. Move anywhere on that car and you are fine, or even jump to the next car. It is all right so long as you move to anything moving at the same progression. But try and step off that car while it is moving and you are left in the dust. The car speeds out of sight. Your world has gone. You are now in a different progression. You can't get back until you accelerate fast enough to overtake that car.

Einstein postulated that a curvature of space would cause even light to bend through it? an electromagnetic wavelength that traditionally follows straight lines. Maverick idea. But in 1919 Sir Arthur Eddington detected a change in a star's position during a total eclipse. Einstein seemed to be right: space was curving around the planet, and light was being bent. He was awarded his doctorate, which in part read cautiously "for adding significantly to the body of theoretical physics. . ." Relativity would not be mentioned, as nobody was sure what that was.

So it seemed space indeed was curving around masses in Space. If this was gravity or the result of gravity, no one is still sure. But if light were affected, it seemed too that other or all energy wavelengths might be affected. After all, light is only an electromagnetic wavelength. If light was curving, then it was slowing. Might the same be true of space? Then if time and space were continuous, might it then also be true of that greatest mystery...Time? Could we slow time by bending space?

The cornerstone of Einstein's Relativity was, of course, $E = mc^2$, that is, energy equals mass times the speed of light squared. It is actually a simple equation, but its ramifications are monumental and universal. It means that there is an incredible amount of energy in any object, if we could just get at it in the nucleus of its atoms. If this could be verified, it would seem to mean that Relativity's basic tenants of space and energy and time being continuous would be one step closer to fact.

It would be by the nuclear detonations at Alamogordo, New Mexico, July 16, 1945, that $E = mc^2$ would be proved. A chain reaction in the uranium atom caused the greatest explosion man had ever known. The atomic age had dawned. As the space age dawned, further proof came of Einstein's concept of the continuity of time and space. Atomic clocks placed at orbital heights recorded time passing just slightly faster than those at sea level. Where gravity, and hence a curvature of space, was greatest time moved more slowly; where it was not, more quickly. The passage of time as we record and experience it here was actually slower than in space.

Mass, such as this planet, did seem to bend space before it, and with this it did seem to slow time. Fractionally, granted. But it finally opened the labyrinth of time to logical conquest. Theoretically, it was proposed the greater the curvature of space, the greater time would be slowed. But if the Earth could only slow time fractionally by is massive size and speed through space, what "on earth" or anywhere else could bend space even more to significantly affect the progression of time?

Now, in the above examples of speeding cars obviously they cannot go fast enough to truly bend space and lock one into a different progression of time. But would it really require huge mass and speed to do it? The planet was indeed doing it slightly. But if time's pathway lay along energy, could not bending or changing its electromagnetic frequencies also bring this about? There must be other methods to bend electromagnetic wavelengths.

ATOMIC CLUE

We must first begin with the atom, any atom. There are only a little over 100 atoms in all the Universe that we know of. All that we see is built out of these and out of a combination of these. All atoms are made up of protons, electrons and neutrons, except hydrogen which has no neutron. No atom is different than the other except in number: Helium, Calcium, Titanium, Tin, whatever; they are all the same thing . . .except in number. They follow an orderly mathematical progression. Hydrogen, the simplest atom, has 1 proton in the nucleus and 1 electron in orbit. Helium has 2; 3 protons in the nucleus and 3 electrons in orbit is no longer a gas; it is Lithium, a silver-while metal. It goes on and on to Seaborgium, with 106 protons in the nucleus.

Therefore, the difference between all matter must be the electromagnetic energy created by the different number of these charged particles, not in the basic make up of these particles as individuals. The reason Nitrogen and

LEVITATION AND INVISIBILITY

Oxygen are such different gases cannot be that Nitrogen has 7 protons and 7 electrons and that Oxygen has 8 of each; it must be in the different amount of electromagnetic energy that that one proton and one electron make that changes the substance.

The difference is not in the makeup of the particles, but in the space between the particles in orbit (electrons) and the nucleus (with protons). That space is the substance of everything. That space is electromagnetic energy. That space is "reality." That space is the atom. Electromagnetism is the substance of everything. In essence, that "space" is the substance of all structure. That space is energy.

Understanding the structure of all matter is fundamental to understand the limitless potential of manipulating or warping electromagnetism, since by doing so you are capable of affecting the very energy that creates all things. This is far superior to the mere splitting of the nucleus of a complex atom. That only provides a violent form of energy. Within the electromagnetic force of the atom is the key to everything: creation, transmutation . . .limitless power.

Single atoms of five common elements: Hydrogen; Carbon; Nitrogen; Oxygen; and Iron. Not only does the varying number of protons in the nucleus and the varying number and system of orbits of electrons make one substance different from the other, the proximity of one type of atom to another creates an unlimited array of substance.

Water molecule H_2O. In other words, 2 atoms of Hydrogen and 1 atom of Oxygen. Two gases combine to make a liquid. It is not a material difference: the protons are still protons, the electrons still electrons. Electromagnetic energy has been affected by the proximity of these charged particles making up the atoms. A new substance is created.

TRANSMUTATION

Radioactive decay. The means by which one elements becomes another. The isotope Uranium 238 (92 protons and 146 neutrons in its nucleus) is unstable, meaning it sheds these particles from its nucleus. Doing so, the vital loss of these protons and neutrons changes it to another substance: a lesser complex one. In this decay chain Uranium changes eventually to common and stable Lead.

The loss of these particles obviously means the change in the electromagnetic force of the atom in question. Losing some of its 92 protons requires that it shed the equal number of electrons. It becomes a less complex atom eventually such as lead, where the process stops. Transmutation is the result of the electromagnetic energy changes that result. In this we can see the power contained in the electromagnetic forces that bind the atom, created by the various particles, their systems of orbit and their number.

Most substances, fortunately, aren't like Uranium 238. They are stable and do not decay. But the example of radioactive decay shows us the power of changing the electromagnetic energy of any atom. If we could do so, then we could effectively carry on any form of transmutation we want.

This must be the basis behind the success of the Hutchison Effect. There can be no other proposal. To render items invisible, at other times transmute them from one substance to another, make objects levitate, burn white hot but not melt surrounding flammable material, or make things "cold melt," fuse, or disappear, can only be because the atoms of that particular substance and the particular frequency each one has, was interrupted or warped, while the other substances, being on a different frequency (due to the different number of charged particles therein) were unaffected. This is limitless power . . . if harnessed repeatedly.

What potential exists within nature to create these electromagnetic changes or bend them in such a sense that it imitates bending of space? How intense does it need to be to cause something we today consider "supernatural" or impossible? Now we get to the Triangle and to the reports of electromagnetic anomalies and aberrations, disappearances, disintergrations? the crux of its infamous mystery. Are these indicators that electromagnetic aberrations are occurring for some unknown reason?

Underscoring the above is crucial to understanding a space warp.

SPACE WARP

The atom is often likened to a "mini solar system, most of it space." It is always surprising to realize that this is true, that the structure of the atom is energy in a confined space between revolving charged particles. Since everything is made of atoms, everything in this Universe is mostly energy, not materially particulate. The electrons, protons and neutrons are only a small part of the atom. It is the space between them that is, ironically, the "substance." Space in this case filled with electromagnetic energy.

Therefore all matter is not only mostly energy, but it is mostly space. This is hardly philosophy disguised as science. This is simple fact. In the above example of the red blood cell, we noted the number of each atoms. This translates to 102,408 charged particles making up the atoms of its structure. These same particles are what is in your computer key board, a wall, a car, rubber, anything. The red blood cell is different because of their arrangement.

LEVITATION AND INVISIBILITY

This creates the red blood cell. Remove the space from that red blood cell and no microscope will be able to detect those tiny particles.

It is the same for everything. Remove the space from it, and you have very little.

It is possible to estimate how many charged particles are in any given substance. Simply consider there are 30,000,000,000 red blood cells in the body. Mathematically, it is possible to determine how many electrons and protons and neutrons make up the blood. Add the volume of all tissues, of every atom from calcium to Iron, to whatever. It is beyond number probably. Take all the space out of the human body and all these charged particles would form a pile that is still so small it is invisible.

The same for a wall? if you know the volume of wood, plaster, etc., and you know the atoms that are the building block of these substances. You can then calculate how many charged particles are in an 8 x 10 wall. Remove the space from a wall and the combined particles might not even form a pellet the size of a small baby aspirin. In other words, take the space out of everything and what you have left isn't much.

If all is mostly space, why can't one substance pass freely through another? Go ahead and run to a wall. You won't go through. It's been tried. It doesn't work. It is not, however, a collision of particles which prevents you from walking through; it is a collision of forces. The atoms of our body: hydrogen, oxygen, nitrogen, calcium, zinc, iron, whatever, are the same as those in the wall; they are in tune, on the same frequency. They are mutually interactive. It is not possible to break the forces . . . or is it?

An electric current is nothing more than electron particles traveling along in the same direction, usually along a wire. These are the same very tiny particles that make of the key elements of every atom: they are the ones whose tremendously speedy revolutions around the atomic nucleus, and by their number and their speed, help to create the energy of each substance.

If I were to take 1,000,000 volts of high frequency electricity (at 60 cycles alternating current) and pass it through my body to ground there is no question I would look like Ramses' mummy in short order. I would be instantly killed. The trillion, trillions, countless trillion and giga trillions of electrons would destroy my whole body .... Remember, 1 ampere measurement of electric energy is equal to 63.3 billion billion electrons per second at any given point of the current. That's a lot of electrons in 1 million volts of high frequency electricity!

But change the frequency of that electricity. Change it to 65,000 cycles, and you can channel that 1 million volts through your body and out your fingertips like lightning . . . if metal thimbles are provided to allow a point of discharge. No? . . . Yes, very true.

The question was put to science long ago. In 1952, Dr. Irwin A. Moon, director of the Moody Institute of Science, demonstrated the reality of it, as have others. I use his example here since he was actually using it in terms of what we would today call a space warp.

The 1950s was full of such talk and examples, as we were entering the exciting age of the atom and all the new knowledge on the structure of the Universe it gave us. Unfortunately, we have forgotten the brilliant pioneers of that age. Today, we think of science only in terms of what monetary advantage its studies can give us. But the world of science is the world of discovery and adventure. And it is this world which is giving firm foundation to such things as time and space warps.

Since Einstein said "Science is merely the refinement of everyday thinking," Let's consider for a moment the above example.

Did it dawn on you? The same particles that make up any wall (anything period), Dr. Moon channeled through his body. The electrons passed through harmlessly . . . though I don't recommend anybody doing this test at home. What he did was merely to change the frequency. The very same particles that are key to giving a wall its atomic stability passed freely through him. If we could change the frequency of the entire atom and not just the charged electron particle, what would be the potential? Could one not pass freely through a wall? What if there was another system of atoms that are not mutually interactive with ours? Could there not be another whole world? Like adjusting the position of a hologram card, would another whole scene emerge if you could manipulate electromagnetism and then the atom onto frequencies we have not yet discovered?

The work of John Hutchison makes one wonder what the potential in nature is, especially over the ocean, to create electromagnetic aberrations that may have frightening results.

One thing is common then to all the Universe: to all reality ? electromagnetic energy. If Einstein was right, it would seem time and space ? hence matter ? are all connected. If a changeover of space could be accomplished by electromagnetism, could the same be the pathway to Time?

TIME WARP

All atoms are in vortex kinesis, as it was stated at the beginning. Therefore all matter is as some level of vortex kinesis. Since it is the nature of matter, anything that might cause a change in this intensity might bring about surprising changes indeed.

We already know that the great spinning orb of the Earth, and its great mass, affects time fractionally at the surface as compared to orbital heights. Time is slowed slightly. But what if we could increase the speed at which the Earth spun, fast enough to even bend space more before it? Could we then not slow time even more? It would seem so. But it is impossible to do that. The Earth is too great a mass for us to manipulate. But warping frequencies into a dangerous spinning vortex may not be as difficult.

A vortex may be the only way because it is spinning energy, an intensified example of the natural state of any matter.

Interestingly, like Elijah's "fiery whirlwind," could such a vortex bring about different progressions of time, different exchanges of space by changing the frequency of the atoms in the area? An energy vortex, like a magnetic vortex, would have unlimited potential on the wavelengths around this planet since it would disrupt them first. One would not have to waste time trying to bend them with a huge atomic mass like a planet.

One example of an energy vortex on the force fields of this Earth may come from the eye of a hurricane. Gravity anomalies have been reported recently. These should not surprise anyone considering the vast swirling energy of a hurricane is centered at its imploding vortex core. But this is a massive atmospheric vortex, like a tornado. No one can get close enough without being obliterated (usually). How could anything experience a time or space anomaly before being destroyed?

Unlike all the atmospheric energy required to start and maintain a hurricane or tornado, magnetic vortices are the result of changes and shifts within the magnetic field of the Earth, deep within its mantel and core. These vortices are definitely believed to swirl into and out of existence within the body of the Earth.

The recent invention of Dr. Evgeny Podkletnov certainly underscores the potential of a natural magnetic vortex. His device was created at Tampere University Labs, Finland, in 1996. It was nothing more than a superconductor (12 inch diameter) sealed inside an outer metal casing filled with liquid nitrogen. The superconductor was set over three solenoids to magnetically levitate it and start it spinning. The liquid nitrogen in the outer casing was to keep it cool while this superconductor ring spun at several thousand RPM.

The phenomenal result was accidentally discovered. One of the assistants' pipe smoke wafted over the device while it spun at 5,000 rpm. The smoke straight away went to the top of the room where it hovered. It was discovered that gravity had been slightly shielded over the device. In essence, a spinning magnetic field (vortex) affected the most mysterious force field of gravity. Dr. Podkletnov discovered via measurements that there was a funnel of less gravity 12 inches diameter above the machine going through each floor of the building and possibly then out into space. When spun to 25,000 rpm, the device took off on its own.

This alarming relationship of gravity to a spinning magnetic field opens the door for future discussions of time and space. Gravity is essential to everything, especially this subject. We are unaware of different time progressions because we all live within the same pull of gravity, cocooning the same progression of time. It is not possible to experience another progression of time or space independent of a field of gravity that is centric to it, in other words, goes with it. Gravity is essential. Gravity may be more than just bending space, but the exact curvature of key energy frequencies that become pulled into the area of the mass, like a planet, or are attracted to the great energy of all of its combined atoms.

In the above example of speeding cars, they can never go fast enough to bend space and slow time. The simple reason is they are within the Earth's gravity. At those speeds any person inside would have to be removed from the seat with a putty knife. This is because the car is accelerating, not the people. They are pushed back by the force of acceleration because the Earth's gravity is greater, and the Earth is not moving at the speeds of a machine going near light-speed.

But if these cars were in their own gravitational field, they could experience unlimited speed and another progression of time. If they could generate the energy to bend and disrupt all of our wavelengths, they may truly experience a very different world than ours.

Gravity is essential, both its creation and disruption. The Sun has gravity, but so does the Earth. Therefore, our tempo is set by the Earth's pace, not the Sun's. The Earth is a pocket of separate gravity than the Sun. To be independent of the Earth's tempo, we must create a field independent of the Earth. So far, however, gravity has eluded us.

Gravity is more than simple attraction. It is orientation. With time, with space there must be gravity of some kind. Even the solar system is tempered by the heliosphere? the gravitational field of our sun. The "void of space" in our solar system is a lie. There are billions of wavelengths whose tempo may be set by the sun's gravity, bent by planets, upset by several interactions, just like the mini solar system of the atom. It is interesting to note that when Pioneer 10, Pioneer 11 and Ulysses left the solar system, the last NASA could detect of them was "an incomprehensible acceleration." They left the gravitational pull of the sun, and in the smooth ocean of wavelengths in intergalactic space they took off. How fast does light travel out there? How fast does time flow? One day we will know. But first we must understand all is energy. This is the blueprint to conquest and exploration. Nothing is impossible.

If gravity is not a curvature of space only, then it is a force within mass. As such it too is tied up in the atom. It becomes the conduit which directs the force of energy. It reflects order, not chaos; it tempers the progression of all things. It orients all things towards itself.

What is the potential in a natural magnetic vortex to affect gravity, time and space? Have they really been discovered in the Bermuda Triangle? Can they come from other sources? Is all this great power and spinning really needed to affect time, or have other, very week electromagnetic tests and warpings been done to show phenomenal things can be done just by interlocking electromagnetic fields, like in the Hutchison Effect?

PARANORMAL LEVITATION AND UFOs

"The amazing source of UFO propulsion is found right here on Earth." That's the incredible revelation of Ken Behrendt in his book, **The Physics of the Paranormal**. Ghosts, alien starcraft, and all manner of paranormal phenomena draw energy from the "anti-mass field" – a bizarre transdimensional source of clean, cheap, renewable energy – discovered by Behrendt.

"I developed the 'anti-mass field theory' to account for UFO propulsion and secondary effects over the course of a 20-year study involving thousands of cases in detail, and tens of thousands of cases in summary. I discovered that a UFO, when airborne, is able to negate its normal gravitational and inertial mass because it contains a device I call an 'anti-mass field generator.' Its purpose is to emit a form of NON-electromagnetic radiation which I call 'anti-mass field radiation.' This new form of radiation has a 'polarity' opposite to that of normal 'mass field radiation' emitted by the subatomic particles that compose the atoms of ordinary matter.

"When these two forms of non electromagnetic radiation -- one from the UFO's propulsion equipment, the other from the subatomic particles that compose the craft and its crew – are superimposed as they radiate away from their sources, they neutralize each other. The result is that the UFO and its crew become massless and, thus, have no weight or inertia. They will float due to buoyancy in a planet's atmosphere, and can violently accelerate and maneuver without damage to the craft and its crew if propulsive forces are applied to the craft's hull."

LEVITATION AND INVISIBILITY

Behrendt believes his "anti-mass field theory" explains a variety of paranormal phenomena, such as levitation.

"In studying levitation, it became apparent to me that, under certain circumstances, the human body could act as a sort of 'biological anti-mass field generator.' In this state, certain religious people have, over millennia, been witnessed to float without visible means of support. I believe that in these cases, the necessary anti-mass field radiation is emitted from the person's circulatory system when certain biophysical conditions are achieved."

Behrendt describes levitation as among the oldest of documented paranormal phenomena, citing a case in the 13th or 14th century A.D. when someone levitated for the Spanish king and his court.

"Those who witnessed it stated that the person who levitated was as light as a soap bubble, and could be blown about by witnesses, This implies not only buoyancy, but an extreme reduction in bodily mass. This is similar to what UFOs do. Some craft engage in the so-called 'falling leaf' motion, wherein the craft sinks slowly in the atmosphere, and rocks to and fro like a plate sinking in water. This is only possible with an extreme reduction in the mass of the craft. (I think in these cases, the craft's crew do this maneuver on purpose, to give earthly witnesses a hint as to how the craft functions.)"

Behrendt is more confident that his anti-mass field theory explains UFOs than levitation.

"While I am sure about the reality of UFOs and anti-mass field generators, I must hypothesize that a human undergoing auto levitation emits anti-mass field radiation (through some natural biological process, since we don't have mechanical anti-mass field generators built into our bodies)."

UFO ABDUCTEES OFTEN REPORT LEVITATION

Alien abductees often report two types of levitation experiences. Some recall being levitated towards a UFO by a dazzling beam of light. In his book *Alien Identities: Ancient Insights into Modern UFO Phenomena* (1993), Richard Thompson writes that, "Psychical phenomena that typically occur during UFO encounters include telepathic communication, levitation, passing of matter through matter, and mysterious healing" (p.161).

The second category of paranormal phenomena that abductees experience occurs after their initial abduction: remembering that many people eventually discover that they are repeat abductees. This generally involves something that resembles poltergeist activity, which some researchers call Electrical Sensitive Syndrome because it appears to be partially electromagnetic in nature. Professor Kenneth Ring describes this in his book ***The Omega Project*** (1992). Apart from effects like causing street lights to go out, there may be spooky examples such as an abductee's CD player switching itself on in the middle of the night, playing that person's favorite song and then turning itself off. Occasionally however, abductees may experience gravitational rather than electromagnetic anomalies during which they find themselves spontaneously levitating. In his book ***Dimensions: A Casebook of Alien Contact*** (1990, p.176), Jacques Vallee gives an example of a French doctor to whom this occurred.

There is a third levitation connection with ufology. In an article called "The Entities" in the MUFON Journal (1994, p.3), Dan Wright, who was then the manager of the MUFON Abduction Transcription Project, tells us that forty-one percent of the project's abduction transcripts that mention how aliens move, describe them as levitating or gliding. Is it possible that some aliens have mastered the esoteric art of levitation and use it to move themselves and abductees around when in unfamiliar gravitational conditions? If this is so, we perhaps have an additional reason for researching levitation more seriously than has been done in the past.

SCIENCE OR MYSTICISM?

One way to find useful clues as to how human levitation might work is to analyze what the various groups that occasionally produce such reports have in common. Several connections are obvious. A belief in spirits and/or a spiritual realm is integral to shamanism, mysticism, spiritualism, spirit possession and poltergeist activity. Although such beliefs do not actually amount to proof that spirits and a spirit realm actually exist, they do suggest that something is going on; but what?

The people who belong to these groups often enter trances or altered states of consciousness æ either voluntarily or involuntarily æ and many of them develop paranormal abilities other than levitation. This introduces the closely related and often controversial subjects of parapsychology and consciousness research, which will be discussed later. Alien abductions also have several interesting similarities with these groups.

Many abduction experiences closely resemble shamanic initiation experiences. Like shamans, abductees often develop an animistic perspective in which they see aliens as a type of spiritual being from another realm or dimension. They may also develop various paranormal abilities, including healing. Like some shamans this may involve the ability to look into a person's body and diagnose illness, almost as if they had x-ray vision.

LEVITATION AND INVISIBILITY

An animistic perspective also involves a deep concern for animals and the environment. Abductees may start to see Earth as if it were alive and in desperate need of better treatment than it is getting at present. This raft of feelings is perhaps best documented by Professor John Mack in **Passport to the Cosmos** (2000).

Another interesting similarity between shamanism and alien abductions is that in indigenous societies it is often believed that malevolent spirits can kidnap people's souls, thus causing them illness. It is the unenviable role of the shaman to venture into the otherworld and retrieve the soul, thus restoring the patient to health. Similarly, alien abductees can be referred to an abduction counselor because they appear to be suffering symptoms of post-abduction stress, yet are unable to recall what has happened to them. In a sense we could say that their memories of what happened to them have also been abducted.

Somewhat like a shaman, the therapist are often using hypnosis æ ventures into the abductee's unconscious to help retrieve those lost memories and restore the patient to health. We could speculate, therefore, that the difference between a person's unconscious and the shamanic otherworld might simply be a matter of cultural terminology æ they may actually be largely the same thing, which again brings us back to consciousness research.

There are a few religious groups who claim that aliens are actually demonic entities intent on corrupting or subverting the human race. In other words, they believe that alien abductions are a form of spirit possession. This is a delicate subject, but there is no doubt that many abductees report that initially they are completely unable to prevent or resist their abduction experiences. It is as if their body and/or consciousness has been taken over by a force greater than themselves. Repeat abductees may become more relaxed about their experiences and may even look forward to further encounters, while others report becoming familiar with various aliens and being able to negotiate the circumstances of future encounters.

If we think about this, we can see that there is not that much difference between, firstly, a shaman learning to interact with or be temporarily possessed by beings from the spirit realm, and, secondly, a spirit medium allowing the spirit of a dead person to temporarily inhabit his or her body during a séance. In some cases both these are similar to someone being abducted or interacting with an alien who has paranormal or spiritual qualities from some seemingly spiritual or interdimensional realm. The difference may be largely a matter of cultural definition and can perhaps be measured by how much control the shaman, spirit medium, or abductee has, or learns to have, over the initial and subsequent encounters. In indigenous societies a person who cannot get rid of a spiritual entity that has possessed him or her is regarded as mad rather than as a shaman. Likewise, in Christianity for example, a person who becomes involuntarily possessed and starts to display paranormal abilities and/or levitates is definitely not regarded as a saint, although some saints claim to have encounters with spiritual beings and may also levitate.

Historical accounts suggest that some mystics were most reluctant to reveal instances of spontaneous levitation in case they were thought to be possessed. The Catholic researcher Olivier Leroy in his book ***Levitation: An Examination of the Evidence and Explanations*** (1928) makes it quite plain that he believes that saints that levitate are divinely blessed, while spirit mediums are just being duped by demonic entities. Leroy is clearly biased, but one wonders what he would have thought about alien abductions if he were still alive.

The Catholic church's apparent ambivalence about miraculous phenomena makes human levitation harder to investigate because it reduces the number of witnesses and subsequent documentation of such events. For example, the Croatian stigmatist Father Zlatko Sudac, who visited America early in 2002, claims to have "the gifts of levitation, bilocation, illumination, and the knowledge of upcoming events." However, when asked about them during a recent interview, he declined to elaborate until the Catholic hierarchy had made a pronouncement about the matter.

A variation on religious ambivalence is the poor documentation of miraculous events in cultures where paranormal abilities are taken for granted. Such a blasé attitude is illustrated by a story about the Tibetan yogi Milarepa (1052-1135) who is reported to have once levitated over the heads of some distant relatives who were plowing a field.

The man's son spotted the levitating monk and called to his father to stop work and observe the miracle. Milarepa's relative looked up, saw the levitating holy man, and firmly instructed his son to ignore that "good-for-nothing" and get back to work.

THE HUTCHISON EFFECT

Starting at a very young age, John Hutchison has been fascinated by machines. He had an empathy for them–machine tools, guns, steam engines, and most of all, electromagnetic and physics gear. Being somewhat reclusive, Hutchison had a lot of time to work and play with a variety of devices. The electronics experiments of his childhood would blaze during the dark Canadian winter nights, much to the chagrin of his nearby neighbors. He even became somewhat of a celebrity when the local newspaper ran an article about

LEVITATION AND INVISIBILITY

his home electronics laboratory. After Hutchison moved away from his parents home, he slowly began to build fill his low-rent basement laboratory with inexpensive surplus and scrap yard equipment. He made money doing odd jobs such as repairing electronic devices and gunsmithing. He even hand-wound huge wire coils for the generators. Most of his money was spent on duplicating Nikola Tesla's remarkable spark-gap experiments, which he did in almost total isolation.

One day, in 1979, Hutchison turned on his Tesla coils, radio-frequency generators, static generators, and a host of other devices all at once to study possible field interactions between my equipment. Suddenly, a bar of steel that was on the floor floated a few feet up in the air. After a few seconds, it fell to the floor with a bang.

Hutchison was mystified and wondered if this was some new phenomenon due to his odd combination of equipment. Or had he been hallucinating? The next day turned turned on the same equipment, put steel bars in what he thought was the same place...but nothing happened.

Hutchison continued his experiments. Once a glass insulator levitated about two feet into the air. Another time, it was a saw. Yet, the results were sporadic and he could never tell from one day to the other what was going to happen. He labored to exactly duplicate the voltages, currents, microwave flux, and placement of equipment, and even studied the order in which each machine was turned on. With a variety of equipment–panoramic spectrum analyzer, magnetometer, Geiger counters, and other detectors–Hutchison monitored the events, hoping to figure out an explanation for the levitation.

it was clear that he needed help from "real" scientists. So he went to a meeting of physicists in Vancouver and talked about his findings. There he met Mel Winfield who became interested in what Hutchison was doing. Winfield was the first physicist to visit the lab and photograph objects floating in the air. He displayed the photos and discussed Hutchison's work at another physics meeting.

Through the Pharos Company, Hutchison's work received support from the U.S. Army and Navy. He brought in witnesses, including scientists from the U.S. and Canadian defense departments, Los Alamos National Laboratory, and various corporations, including Boeing, and they saw material levitating in the lab. In fact, some people even made videos of the weird results.

Sometimes metal would break up with a strange fracturing. At Siemens Corporation, and other company, university, and government labs, experts examined materials that had undergone such breakage, and found unusual microscopic and macroscopic structures. Unfortunately, it is difficult to find any scientific conclusions based on this research. Possibly no one wants to be associated with something that is considered "fringe science." Another possibility is that this research has gone "dark," taken over by military agencies who are looking into possible weapons applications for the Hutchison Effect.

Hutchison's lab contained almost 20 tons of equipment. Ranging from Tesla coils, radar generators, signal generators, pulse generators, and phase inverters. It looked like the inside of a 1940 warship with a Frankenstein-making lab in the center.

Hutchison carefully removed equipment that wasn't needed and the levitation repeatability improved. His research also helped to determine where each piece of equipment needed to be in relation to the target material.

What exactly is the Hutchison Effect? No one, not even John Hutchison, knows for sure. The power was transformed to signal generators, radar systems, broadband systems, high voltage systems, and magnetic pulsed coils. These energies overlapped in a specific area where the item was to be levitated or the material transformed. Presumably, the effect works at the subatomic level, perhaps related to the zero-point field.

Whatever the science is behind the Hutchison Effect, the results are certainly fascinating. This includes levitation, strange physical changes in metals, and other odd effects. He has somehow gotten totally different materials, like wood and metal, to interpenetrate each other, not by displacement but by some kind of interlacing of their atomic structures.

Several laboratories, from scientifically recognized institutions such as NASA and the Max Planck Institute, have attempted to reproduce his experiments, but so far none has been capable of reproducing his results. In fact John Hutchison himself hasn't been capable of reproducing his own results for a long period of time. He explains that this is because of the great loss of equipment due to the military intelligence service destruction of his lab, or because he has been restricted by the government from doing his experiments. Most scientists assume that his results are a hoax.

Despite having lost much of his original equipment, John Hutchison continues with his experiments. He is not bothered by the skeptics, for he is certain that one day, maybe not in his lifetime, his work will be heralded as the beginning of a whole new understanding of how the universe works. As well, Hutchison hopes that the Hutchison Effect will lead mankind to a brighter future of clean, unlimited energy and possibly even a way to finally move outwards into space and reach for the stars.

LEVITATION AND INVISIBILITY

Send your name and mailing address for our Free Catalog of fascinating books, interesting DVDs, and mind-blowing audio CDs/

GLOBAL COMMUNICATIONS
P.O. BOX 753
NEW BRUNSWICK, NJ 08903

Email: mrufo8@hotmail.com

Visit our website at:

www.conspiracyjournal.com

HERE ARE THE LATEST MYSTICAL SECRETS FROM FAMED HUNGARIAN BORN PSYCHIC MARIA D'ANDREA, REVEALED IN HER NEW BOOK AND VIDEO DRAMATIZATION

COME UP TO THE "GOOD LIFE" WITH MARIA'S TOP ONE DOZEN SPELLS AND OCCULT GALLERY OF MYSTICAL AND SPIRITUAL ESSENTIALS

$24.00 + $5 S/H

Though most popularly known as the "Money Psychic," Hungarian born Maria D' Andrea is actually knowledgeable on a wide range of paranormal topics. Each week she focuses on a different topic in her widely seen TV show The Sprititual World With Maria broadcast throughout Long Island. In addition, she has given lectures and seminars on subjects that are widely diverse.

In her latest work (accompanied by a Free Bonus DVD), **MARIA D' ANDREA'S SECRET OCCULT GALLERY AND SPELL CASTING FORMULARY,** she delves into over fifty little known aspects of the occult. In addition, scattered amongst the pages are twelve of her most powerful spells that she has only shared up until now with her most privileged students.

WHY THIS OCCULT GALLERY IS IMPORTANT TO YOU— TOPICS DISCUSSED

Psychic Self-Defense · How Herbs Relate To Spiritual Work · Energy Streams: Mother Nature's Party Lines · Are You A Modern Day Prophet? Children In The Path Of Light · Manifesting Your Own Future · Utilizing The Power Of Belief · Communicating On A Psychic Level How To Be Guided By Spiritual Realms · The Secret Power Within Crystals And Candles · Journey To Another Plane Earth Changes And How They Affect You · Stones of Intrigue · Living An Alpha Reality · UFOs And Crystals Colored Lights - Effects of Being Exposed To Them · How To Use "Wind Magic" · Choices On Your Path · U.F.O.'s On The Astral Plane Identifing Forms With Power · Lucid Dreams · Ghosts Versus Spirits · Sounds Of Power · Symbolic Magick And Its Many Uses My Invisible Partners · Imagination Versus Psychic: How To Identify · Prosperity And Happiness All Yours! When To Tell You Are Guided By Spirit Beings · Out Of Body Travel Without Baggage · Telepathy: Direct Communication Ghostology: Finding Unseen Forces · The Inner Kingdom · New Age Formulary · Hobgoblins · Ghost Of The Tribes · The Tidra The Link Between Realities · Story Of The Bats · Empowerment Through The Word Influence Of UFOs On Spiritual Awareness · Dreams: Your Direct Phone Line · Dream Pillows · God's Creatures - Our Psychic Connection Psychic Rune Casting to Native Indian Crafts · Universal Lines Of Force · Tree Doctor

Revealed: Maria's Most Powerful Spells Never Published Previously! Easy To Follow And Perform Yourself

SPELL 1 – LOVE AND GOD
SPELL 2 – MANIFEST WITH THE GOD BOX
SPELL 3 — KEEPS NEGATIVITY AWAY
SPELL 4 - SEA MAGIC FOR ANY WISH
SPELL 5 – TO RELEASE ANGER
SPELL 6 – HELP FOR AN ANGELIC SPIRIT
SPELL 7 – SPELLS WITH GODDESS FREYJA
SPELL 8 – TO BRING IN LUCK
SPELL 9 – THE SPELL OF LOVE
SPELL 10 – THE WHIM OF THE GODS SPELL
SPELL 11 – SUCCESS SPELL OF THE DRAGON KINGS
SPELL 12 – HAPPINESS AND HARMONY SPELL

HOW TO ORDER – This remarkable book and study guide with its bonus DVD is bound to enhance your being. If you are looking for success this progressive metaphysical volume is for you. And if you want a great Occult Gallery filled with a wondrous trove of information and facts, send just $24.00 + $5 S/H and request MARIA'S OCCULT GALLERY. It will be a decision you will be happy to have made.

SUPER SPECIAL
5 BOOKS AND 5 DVDS IN AD $99.00 + $10 S/H
TIMOTHY G. BECKLEY · BOX 753
NEW BRUNSWICK, NJ 08903

OTHER BENEFICIAL TITLES BY MARIA D' ANDREA

EACH BOOK COMES WITH A FREE DVD
All books are large format Study Guides
( ) **HEAVEN SENT MONEY SPELLS**
Learn why Maria is known as the "Money Psychc" as she brings prosperity into your life with these easy to do spells. - **$21.95**
( ) **YOUR PERSONAL MEGA POWER SPELLS**
Hundreds of love spells, money spells, spells for protection against negative forces. Enhance your entire being. -- **$25.00**
( ) **OCCULT GRIMOIRE AND MAGICAL FORMULARY**
500 spells to manifest your own future destiny. Benefits of using candles, crystals, herbs. All positive information. - **$25.00**
( ) **SECRET MAGICKAL ELIXIRS OF LIFE**
Turn a glass of water into a powerful elixir for improved good health, enhanced psychic abilities and the fortification of inner strength. - **$25.00**

ALSO AVAILABLE
SPECIALLY PREPARED GEMSTONE KIT
YOU CAN USE WITH MARIA'S BOOKS & DVDS
Contains green agate, amethyst, carnelian, citrine, hematite, green jasper, rose quartz, green quartz, clear quartz, sodalite, and tiger's eye, and a vial of lavender oil and a blue travel bag.
ADD THIS KIT TO YOUR ORDER
FOR JUST $20.00

18013970R00081

Made in the USA
Charleston, SC
11 March 2013